HIRE POWER

USE STRATEGIC RESOURCING TO SHARPEN YOUR COMPETITIVE EDGE

JOHN WALLACE

First Published in Great Britain 2017 by mPowr (Publishing) Limited
www.mpowrpublishing.com

A catalogue record for this book is available from the British Library
ISBN – 978-1-907282-83-6

Design by Martyn Pentecost
mPowr Publishing 'Clumpy™' Logo by e-nimation.com
Clumpy™ and the Clumpy™ Logo are trademarks of mPowr Limited

mPowr Publishing Presents...

When you pick up a book by mPowr Publishing you are in for an adventure. Our passion is transformational content, ideas, stories, tools and strategies that empower lives, businesses and communities. You are not likely to get what you expect but you will always find what you need. We don't do bland, generic information. We celebrate the inner quirk, the outer quest and the joy of building legacies that last. Adventurers, Be Enchanted!

CONTENTS

INTRODUCTION

If you are reading this there is probably something not quite right with resourcing in your business. Perhaps you are concerned about some hiring that hasn't worked out. Perhaps recruitment is a massive drain on the HR budget. Perhaps you aren't getting enough candidates for your jobs. Perhaps you are looking for a fresh view on some of the eternal recruitment questions. How do I attract the best people? What are the best assessment tools? What is the best technology? How can I reduce my time to hire? My cost per hire?

All important questions. However, this is not a book with the quick fix for recruitment problems. You won't get a to-do list of easy steps.

What you *will* get is a challenge to the way that recruitment and resourcing are thought about. It is treated as the critical and empowering business activity that it is. Resourcing to secure future capability, not to put bums on seats cheaply and quickly. The quick fix *how* is enterprise and situation specific. The way to think about *how* is universal.

There is no focus on how to reduce the time it takes to recruit people, or how to reduce the cost of recruitment. There is solely a focus on quality. Getting the people into the business with the right capabilities to take the business in the direction it wants to go. Building a high-performing organisation through a resourcing strategy. Take care of that, and the cost and time to hire targets take care of themselves.

The change to strategic resourcing is, at the same time, both complex and simple.

It is complex because there are lots of moving parts. The flux in a business, the shifting of the markets, economic ebb and flow, the impact of technology and, above everything else, the complexity that comes with something that is always about people. And people are complicated and ultimately largely unpredictable.

Resourcing also happens to be about people in highly emotional situations. People deciding to move on in their career, people playing politics, people making hiring decisions, people selling a service, people exaggerating about their strengths, people making snap decisions, people doing their best, but it's not good enough. People being, well, people.

If you ensure that there are three basic conditions in place then you give yourself a much better chance of resourcing your business with the right skills and great capability. That's what makes its simple.

A *much better chance*. Note—that is not a guarantee. There are no guarantees when it comes to finding the right match between job and person. The complexity ensures there will always be mismatches.

This is a real problem for resourcing. The occasional random fantastic decision will shine and betray poor practice. The practice is perpetuated, and longer-term damage is done. Overall capability will remain static. *Even a blind squirrel finds an acorn once in a while.* Don't be seduced by happy accidents.

Don't focus on outcomes. Focus on the process. Get the simple things right, and let the outcome take care of itself. Don't tear apart a great process for a bad outcome, and don't ignore the bad process for the great outcome. Learn and refine, but if the right conditions are in place trust that the end result will be long-term, sustainable improvement. Resourcing is not about delivering perfect. It is about creating the environment with the highest probability of delivering perfect.

The cumulative outcome of better chances is a tremendous prize. In today's world, people move jobs more frequently than ever, and each promotion, move, leaver and joiner is an opportunity to improve. Scale that up, over time, and the opportunity becomes visible.

Resourcing strategically is shifting from transactional to transformational, in a way no other part of HR can achieve. The final challenge of the book is to move resourcing from the periphery of HR strategy to the centre.

This way of thinking about resourcing is partly illustrated in the book through the trials and tribulations of a fictional entity, Lothian Bank. It is not based at all on any real organisation and is purely a figment of my imagination. As they say in the movies, "Any resemblance to actual persons, living or dead, or actual events is purely coincidental."

What is not imaginary, in the slightest, are the challenges faced in Lothian Bank. There is nothing extreme, hyperbolic, fantastical about any of them. If I haven't seen the failings that exist there with my own eyes, I've certainly had them described to me by another of the resourcing tribe. If anything, reality is worse than fiction.

There are also numerous real life examples and case studies from the real world. These fall into two categories. Stories of *bad stuff* and stories of *good stuff*. In general, I have hidden the identities of the bad stuff companies. This is to protect the very kind sharing of the people who told me the stories. I am keen that they continue to speak to me.

However, *all* the stories are true. There isn't a single iota of exaggeration in any of them. Some minor details have been altered to protect identities, but nothing in the substance. As with the fiction in Lothian Bank, that is simply because there is no need to. Batshit is just too common.

A final point is that there are some topics where I haven't gone into as much depth as I would like. The focus is resourcing strategically for better capability. To maintain that I have simply had to give a passing nod to some important subtopics. I barely touch on diversity, skirt around the variety of operating models, don't debate the merits of recruitment process outsourcing. There is no breakdown of every attraction channel, critique of applicant tracing systems or a list of the ten best assessment techniques. There is much more to be said about graduate recruitment and apprentices.

There is also much thinking to be done and debate to be had about the evolution of work. What are the skills of the future? What are the jobs of the future? What will future generations want from work? What do changing global demographics mean for the workplace? What does automation mean for the workplace? What does globalization mean for the workforce? There is a myriad of macro trends at the present time, all with consequences and all delivering their share of uncertainty. That's for another time.

This book is unapologetically about how important resourcing is. How thinking about future resource is much better than reacting to the present. What the conditions for success need to be. How changes can make a tremendous capability impact in any organisation. How that impact can enhance business performance, and deliver competitive advantage.

I would like to thank all the people who have helped me with their stories. The many who drank coffee, wine and beer with me in active research and the many more over the years who shared their tales and rolled their eyes. Thanks all, you know who you are...

CHAPTER I
THE CHALLENGE

"The team with the best players wins."

Jack Welch

Having skilled people in place at the right time makes all the difference in business. Failing to get the right people, or failing to get people at all is crippling. Those two statements are obvious. So why does it seem so hard? Why does all the evidence suggest that getting the right people is a constant headache for so many? Why isn't resourcing seen as a priority?

Do you have critical gaps in your business? Are there areas where you are crying out for people but they just aren't there? Positions that stop customer service, production, sales or present a regulatory or financial risk? Do you understand what your capability

1

or resource shortfalls really are? What is the impact? Do you have a strategic resourcing strategy to meet these gaps?

If you have gaps, or people with inadequate capability, you are leaving yourself exposed to the risk of ambush by issues you don't know exist. In the modern world, with rapidly evolving skill requirements and a more mobile workforce, just bumping along as before is blindly accepting that risk. More than ever, businesses need to think about resourcing in a strategic way. Not about hiring when the ambush is sprung, but understanding and coordinating resourcing to deliver the right people, doing the right things at the right time.

There's real risk in not focusing on resourcing. There's real benefit in the right strategy. Why isn't everyone all over this?

The latest PWC Chief Executive Officer (CEO) annual survey puts the problem in sharp relief. 87% of CEOs are extremely worried about finding people with the right skills. 85% particularly struggle to hire the right leadership skills. It isn't just PWC saying this. Any list of top business issues will tell you the same thing. This is also not a new problem. A list from ten or twenty years ago would paint precisely the same picture.

Management consultants have produced many reports and papers on key skills shortages. Recruitment advertising agencies and recruitment consultants have talked for years about the *war for talent*. Against this backdrop, the only conclusion is that finding and keeping the right people is a problem, has been a problem and looks set to continue being a problem.

If we know it's a problem that significantly negatively impacts business performance, why isn't addressing the resourcing and capability issues right at the forefront of the organisational agenda? Most companies will state that people are their biggest asset, or some other sentiment acknowledging that their employees are the reasons behind their successes and, by extension, their failures. Where is the strategic focus? Who is winning the war for talent, if 87% think they aren't?

Nobody is. There is no war for talent. That expression has become an accepted truth, but it presents a misleading view of the problems, which doesn't help form the right solution. It is evocative of a struggle for a few talented individuals who will make or break your business. It suggests a need for urgency and aggression in a chaotic battlefield. That's not what your business needs. You want to secure the right people for your organisation in the right place at the right time. You want the right capability in place when you need it. It is not about conflict, it is about being thoughtful in approach and planning. It is not viewing the business of resourcing as a series of tactical skirmishes for those gifted few. It is solving a problem of understanding and delivering the right resourcing mix for your business, now and in the future.

What is the resourcing mix? Getting the best out of a business boils down to putting the right people doing the right jobs. An internal move. A promotion, or planned move for someone of high potential. Hired from the outside world. Headhunted from a competitor. Temporary or permanent. A process entirely outsourced to a third party. Indeed, with advances in technology, the future resourcing mix will include the option of automation for many more roles.

There are fundamental flaws in *organisation thinking* about what resourcing is, or why it is important. That flawed thinking then extends to delivery. To have the best chance of getting the right people, with the right skills in the right place at the right time, that flawed thinking needs to be challenged.

Lothian Bank is a mid-sized bank, with a retail footprint, head office functions and a scattering of contact centres. It offers full service banking for personal customers and has big plans to expand and consolidate its online presence. It is one of the *challenger* banks, breaking the stranglehold of the big PLC banks.

As James, the CEO, was travelling home after another challenging day in the office, he reflected on how things were going.

His day had started with a difficult meeting involving the financial regulator. Some of the customer interactions on the bank's mortgage products weren't quite what they should have been. Processes were irritatingly out of date, and some important data in the customer application process had been regularly missed. He had wanted his director of mortgages to manage the meeting with the regulator by himself, but he had a sneaking suspicion that the guy would feel the pressure and wouldn't quite get the right result. Unfortunately, his suspicions were confirmed in the meeting as James needed to jump in a few times to make sure the regulators went away satisfied that the remedial plan was in place.

He had also spoken at length with his chief information officer (CIO) about the troubling news that one of their competitors had their current account systems hacked and customer data stolen. He'd read reports about it throughout the day and wanted reassurance from the CIO that it couldn't happen to them. The CIO was honest and fairly confident they were safe. *Fairly* wasn't exactly what James wanted to hear.

Then there was the ongoing deteriorating customer service level which hovered consistently below target. Customers were hanging on the phone for too long trying to get through to customer service. The online chat functionality that was supposed to ease the pressure just wasn't having an impact. To date there had been no telling effect on customer attrition, but he'd been in the business for long enough to know that it was just a matter of time. People only put up with bad service for so long.

The problems were minor, but they all just pulled back from the performance he wanted. Each was small, but there was a cumulative effect and it frustrated him hugely. Two things particularly nagged him. Firstly, all the issues were avoidable. Secondly, they might indicate a deeper threat to the overall health of the organisation. A real concern, given that the problems were all about people. James always considered himself to have real focus on his staff. If they had people problems for all these minor things, could they really kick on with their ambitions?

The doubts about his director of mortgages had bubbled for a while, and it was this instinct that guided him to provide the extra support today. The man was relatively new to the firm, and James was sure there was lots of potential there, but after six months he should really be flying. Instead he was struggling. Soon, this would be apparent to the team beneath him, just as it was becoming clear to his peer group. That could finish him at the firm. James reflected that in hiring him they didn't quite account for the fact that he was moving from the number two and successor in a bigger business to join them, and there would be a lot of adjusting to a smaller firm and different politics. Right from day one, they didn't know how he would react in the politics of a bigger leadership role in a smaller business. Those doubts were well founded and now they had to invest disproportionate time and effort in support and air cover.

The problem in the contact centre was just one of a never-ending stream of similar issues. The director of customer service reported that the lack of first-time call issue resolution was the main problem. Although they were at full headcount there were more temporary staff than planned in the centres, as permanent hiring was difficult. She was careful not to blame her HR colleagues, and talked about the *market*. Seemed a convenient excuse. The problem with so many temporary staff was that they just didn't have the time to fully train them. They then couldn't handle more complex calls, or use the system properly. That just heaped more pressure on the team leaders and experienced permanent staff. Everyone was frazzled.

As for the concerns about cybersecurity, James reflected that they had just addressed a demand to bolster that team to meet the change in online customer behaviour too late in the day. It was surprisingly tough to get good people with that specific skill set. All their growth was online and it frustrated him that they were slow out of the blocks to build the security to protect that critical area. As he arrived home, it became clear that all of the problems he had been dealing with had a basis in a failure to get the right people, or a failure to get people at all. That was irritating. Such a simple miss.

In fact, as he thought longer about it and processed all the issues he could think of, every single one was down to the same thing.

The delayed new website launch last year. That was all because they underestimated how difficult the digital skills were to find.

Then there was the rebuilding of his executive team due to expansion and a couple of shock resignations. However, it was apparent that there simply wasn't the pool of capable people to step up in the business. It was all external hiring and that took up so much time. Why weren't people thinking about successors properly? Isn't that a fundamental of leadership?

There were then a couple of senior hires he had signed off, as he built the team, that simply weren't right. He put that down to too much senior recruitment in a short period of time. He winced though as he thought that maybe his instincts in finding leaders wasn't quite what he thought. He had always backed his judgement when it came to people, but perhaps its wasn't as reliable as he thought. He felt uncomfortable that his own actions had contributed to the issues they now faced.

Last year the low take-up of the new credit card, was down to the lack of sales skills in the branch network. Then, there was the overall sloppiness in project delivery across the business, where delays and poor delivery was the norm. A lack of project management skills. A botched branch roll-out was a direct result of that failing.

The list went on.

He resolved to get to a solution. It felt like a tall order. He considered all the moving parts. IT, customer service, the executive team, finance, human resources, etc. Not only complicated, but constantly evolving and changing. No one person who could articulate the reasons for these diverse problems, let alone anyone with a solution. His earlier confidence that these were somehow separate and minor concerns was replaced by the idea that there was a deeper root cause; a malignancy across the business. The inability to have the right people in place was hurting them badly.

The link between the root cause of so many business problems and resourcing is a very straightforward sequence. Things go wrong because a set of tasks have been completed badly, or not done at all. The tasks that need done to deliver a business plan, or deliver day-to-day business are organised into jobs throughout the organisation. The tasks are the component elements of each job's deliverables. Jobs with a people in them, or not. If there isn't a person in the role, or if the person in the role doesn't have the right skills, then there is the potential for an issue. If there are lots of such occasions of missing or inadequacy, the chances of issues arising is multiplied.

It's simple. Having the right, skilled people in these roles gets the job done and creates business success. Getting them in place is having a resourcing plan. Sometimes though, the link between a failing resourcing approach and business pain is missed.

The experience of Four Seasons, Britain's biggest residential care business for the elderly, illustrates just how damaging resourcing issues can become, and just how that can be missed as the issue.

With an increasingly aging population, social services struggle to cope with the demands placed on them. They rely on the private sector when it comes to elderly care, and the need has never been greater. Companies like Four Seasons, who provide this care nationwide, are very important. They have 440 sites, and look after 18,500 elderly people. They manage this with a total of 18,500 staff.

When Four Seasons suffered an annual loss of some £270 million, despite an aggressive turnaround plan, the future looked bleak. The business sought to sell off properties and, in some locations, it virtually withdrew from the market. The commonplace media diagnosis of the problem was to blame it on a squeeze on income through a reduction in fees from local authorities. They also attributed blame to the changes in the minimum wage for younger staff. This double pressure on income and expenditure makes perfect sense.

The root cause of the problem, however, lay elsewhere. Occupancy for Four Seasons ran at nearly 90%, which is above average for the industry, so the squeeze on income was bearable. Also, their permanent staff costs didn't shift materially because of the changes in the minimum wage. The real wage pressure was with temporary staff.

What really hurt them was an inability to find permanent staff in some critical areas, and as a result they had a very high proportion of temporary agency staff filling roles on a pseudo-permanent basis. In a business where the margins are fine, the critical factor that tipped the business over is that they have struggled to maintain the level of permanent, long-term staff that they need. Maintaining a high level of temporary staff was an unbearable financial burden.

Challenges in resourcing have real and significant business consequences. However, aren't the answers out there in abundance? The internet and LinkedIn are full of helpful guidance. *Five steps to perfect recruitment*, or, *the ten best ways to find that perfect candidate*. The real problem is complex and simple answers won't satisfy. More likely to be five ways to apply a sticking plaster to a gaping wound, or ten ways to mask an issue, without solving it. The number of people who are available to help with resourcing or recruitment and capability and talent is legion. In most organisations of any size there will be lots of good people doing the right things. Aren't these issues just part and parcel of the rhythm of business? Unavoidable?

Perhaps the five things will help a little and that's as good as it'll get? Just part of the ongoing war for talent?

If thinking about resourcing remains the same, then, yes indeed the extent of these challenges will just remain part of the fabric of business. If the thinking changes, then there is a real prize to be won. Don't treat resourcing as a tactical event, think of it as a strategic solution.

Lucy was just starting her career at Lothian Bank as the head of resourcing. The challenges were already mounting. She had just wrapped up her weekly call with Sally, the operations director, and her volume recruitment manager, Mark. They usually talked about the ongoing campaigns and what the plans were. That call, however, had been a very difficult 45 minutes.

As she surveyed her notes it was abundantly clear that Sally was not in a great place, and the recruitment team was starting to feel the heat of her frustration. Mark was the most reliable of Lucy's direct reports, with a great future, and Lucy knew that he was working at full speed to deliver for Sally. However, right now, even with the best will in the world, he was clearly falling short. Lucy had defended him as best she could, but it was just that. Defence. Defence in the face of a pretty justified attack on the level of current delivery. Justified on one level, but at the same time, Lucy felt it was all a little unfair.

True, Mark had fallen short in the numbers expected at the last two assessment centres for telephony staff in the two main contact centres. On the surface, it was simply a fail by the recruitment team. As Sally explained how she had instructed her managers to come off the floor to make sure they were present for the interviews, and that half of them stood around doing nothing for the afternoon, Lucy felt immense frustration. They returned to the floor with reports of a half-empty assessment centre, and poor quality in what few attendees there were. It reflected badly on Mark, Lucy and the HR function. "HR wasting our time… again," she could hear them say.

What made Lucy feel it was all slightly unfair was that Mark was on the back foot from the start because of the sudden jump in permanent staffing requirements from the demand planning team in operations. A sudden *unplanned* jump in requirements caused by a marketing campaign that they were unaware of in HR. That in turn was exacerbated by the high levels of recruitment activity by a couple of competitors, completely changing the market in the location. The location had always been a tough recruitment market. Not where Lucy would have chosen to put a contact centre, but, of course, she would never be asked.

She sighed and dialled Mark's number. Mark would be mortified, and frustrated at the same time. He, better than anyone, knew that weak planning had got them to this point. On the other hand, he also would know that he had dropped a few balls. He would feel better knowing he had Lucy's support. She also resolved to call Sally in the morning. Sally was a great person to work with and really appreciated the work of the recruitment team. If she was venting at them, there was a reason that went beyond Mark's bad day at the office. She suspected that there was an underlying unhappiness with something, but if that was the case she'd prefer it to be out in the open.

After speaking to Mark, Lucy considered the other challenges she was facing. Actually, *challenges* was the nice corporate way of describing the current list of things on her desk. Most of them felt like problems, and all of the problems felt like things she had to get done, but hadn't been given the time or the tools to do them.

Top of the list was the growing crisis with IT recruitment. The change of strategy to focus more on online customer acquisition and online service was the sort of challenge that her manager for IT recruitment relished, but as usual the recruitment team was given the requirements very late in the day. The planning had been done about what the new departments were to do, and what the growth would be, but the movement from concept to actual live recruitment requirements was typically glacial. The recruitment manager for IT recruitment had pushed and pushed, but the time between sign-off and most of the required start dates was unrealistic and put them on the back foot from the off.

What irritated Lucy the most was that this was by no means a new thing, but the heat would be on to deliver. Moreover, she could see trouble coming down the line with this new ask. The fact was the skills that were needed were digital skills and despite a massive effort on LinkedIn the quality coming through was poor. Added to that was the next truth. Banking just wasn't that attractive for the top people in that market and their particular bank was also off the pace when it came to the reward that was required. It all just built the pressure to deliver something that was critical. Lucy knew they would only get the funding they needed once things got really sticky.

It had been exactly the same when they recruited the new cybersecurity team. Huge pressure and a demand for rare skills. Eventually they made all the appointments but not before they had to take a paper to the executive to get the salaries increased. The IT director also harboured doubts about the quality of people that had been brought in, but in the end the managers in that team were basically taking anyone who appeared to have the right technical skills. Organisational fit went right out the door.

The one recruitment issue on her plate that really got under Lucy's skin was the recruitment for the head of credit risk. She was working with the chief risk officer (CRO), who had been vague about what he was looking for and had often proclaimed that he would know the right candidate when he met them. She had already put three highly qualified candidates in front of him, working with a major headhunting firm, and he maintained that he wanted to see *what else was out there.* The headhunters were showing great patience and diligence in continuing to scour competitors, but everyone knew these guys were like hen's teeth in the market and they'd already seen some really good ones. Not only was he being difficult when it came to finding candidates, she knew that she would face other problems as well. When it came to the interviews the CRO had already informed her that he could, "spot a good or a bad candidate in the first five minutes".

As she packed up to leave, she knew that the next few months were going to be tough, and the pressure on the team immense. They would get through, but at the same time Lucy was getting just a little bit tired of just getting through, and right now she needed all the success she could get. She was still new in the job, but had already identified a number of areas that she wanted to change to align to her way of doing things. If she could somehow find a solution to all these problems in front of her, then she would win the mandate for her way of doing things. She wasn't encouraged though. Experience told her that the vacuum created by solving these issues would quickly be replaced by firefighting elsewhere.

The problems faced by Lucy in Lothian Bank are all in a day's work for heads of resourcing. They are faced with inaccurate planning and the pressure for immediate delivery. They deal with constant changes in what they are asked to do. They have constant downward pressure on the cost of their operation. Do more for less. In short, they deal with problems faced by most departmental heads.

However, the resourcing world faces other, unique challenges as well. Resourcing is a tremendously important activity. It can be the difference between success and failure, but for a range of reasons it is only considered so in times of emergency. For a start, the recruitment industry has an image problem.

From zero-hours contracts to inflated headhunting fees, relentless cold-calling and here today, gone tomorrow agencies, the supply side of the recruitment industry often has a poor and unprofessional reputation. This reputation can rub off on the in-house recruitment teams. When it comes to recruitment many of the internal customers already hold a poor perception of the industry and believe that recruitment is an easy, administrative, functional activity. There are few people, outside of the world of recruitment, who see it as a *professional* occupation.

Moreover, HR is often viewed as just a transactional support function—hire, fire, pay, train and policy. The HR director may well be truly respected by their peer group, but it is rare that the HR function is a strategic function. Rightly or wrongly, it is a service function.

The structure of a typical HR department is often a contributing factor. Recruitment is just too often a transactional service, delivered at the point of need. The talent team sit in their own world looking after the career development of a small number of the top people. Internal movement either happens, or not, through circumstance. Contractors and temporary staff are engaged when needed, or when permanent options fail. Graduate programmes are started, and then stopped. It all just *sort of happens*, and people are hired, move, leave, get replaced in a way that sort of advances the business.

As a subset of HR, the resourcing function slides further down the scale. A function that is easy to criticise (after all, everybody can do recruitment), when things go wrong. One that is ripe for budget cutting when things are going along nicely. It's a large budget line in a support function cost centre. It isn't valued. It is transactional. It is siloed. Investment in recruitment is high cost for low return in investment. And, can't everyone just do their own recruitment?

That leads us to the *happy amateurs* who are experts in recruitment. Senior managers have an amazing ability to recall every great hire they have made, but a selective amnesia about the hiring mistakes they have made. Every head of resourcing will know the feeling when they have been asked if they have *ever considered using social media*, or, asked to try *something different*. Everybody is an expert. And when everybody is an expert, then there is no value in expertise.

That's not to say the only knowledge about resourcing and recruitment sits with those who have the subject in their job title. Nor is it to dismiss the notion that managers don't have the critical input into who they hire. They should. What this does show is that recruitment isn't seen as a profession, and its value is then diminished.

Furthermore, it is rare to encounter an HR director with a strong background in resourcing. Recruitment is valued when it doesn't create any *noise* for them with their peers and the CEO. But largely, they tend to spend their time and energy elsewhere. Quite reasonably—diversity, leadership development, executive coaching, reward, management training, managing restructures, well-being initiatives. These are all very worthy issues, and *sexier*. As long as recruitment is a transactional service it remains low on the priority list.

For the head of resourcing this mostly means external recruitment. Often now called *talent acquisition*. The separation of the elements of the resourcing mix creates an immediate problem. The difference between resourcing and recruitment is more than just semantics. James's problem list boils down to concerns about capability or capability and numbers at the right time, in the right place. It's a complex picture and he will struggle to find one person with a view of the whole picture. A head of resourcing's main focus is typically one single element of that whole resourcing mix. Recruitment. The solution only lies in the full picture.

An important activity, business critical, which can make a significant difference but is under-resourced, undervalued, siloed, reactive and transactional. Something not quite right about that.

If we can look at significant business problems and recognise that they have a root in resourcing, and therefore an answer in resourcing, but do not consider resourcing to be a strategic lever, things will never improve. The starting point is recognising that resourcing is important, not just at the point of need, or at the stage when things start to go wrong. It is important in the planning of any business activity.

When Boston Consulting Group conducted a survey to see what HR matters had the most significant impact on the business, they wanted to understand which had the greatest impact on profitability. Delivering on recruitment came out top. That may be because it is a bread-and-butter/must-have/hygiene-factor service. However, it is a hint as to what a real resourcing strategy might achieve.

Sometimes it takes something to have a significant business impact before change will happen.

Virgin Media is a great example of a company who had such an experience, and were willing to make a change. They conducted a net promoter score (NPS) of their recruitment process and some simple arithmetic illustrated a problem. The NPS is a survey of successful and unsuccessful candidates in the process and is a gauge of their experience through the process. Advocates to detractors.

Virgin Media were stunned by the poor NPS results. Of 3,000 survey responses just over half were detractors. That meant that they did enough to significantly annoy more people who applied to them than they didn't.

They knew that 18% of the sample were customers and of those 178 disconnected their Virgin cable service or mobile phone shortly after their recruitment experience. Shortly enough for the link to recruitment to be the reason. They extrapolated that sample to all applications in 2014 and estimated that almost 7,500 customers could have left due to the recruitment experience. An estimated £4.4 million per year.

Needless to say, they made substantial changes and now enjoy a very positive recruitment NPS.

The problems faced by Lucy in Lothian Bank are the embryos of those fully-grown business issues faced by the CEO. They all come down to a gap in capability or just a gap in numbers. What she also sees are the causes and fundamental problems that stop her doing something more strategic. Her function is permanently reactive, relying on unreliable information, or reacting to circumstance. Any resourcing strategy that exists will be a recruitment plan, a so-called strategic plan to deliver tactical needs. However good it is, it will only address immediate problems. Keeping the show on the road.

Making it happen is not easy. The landscape is complex and changing. Your competitors are also looking for good people. Good people have choices. Your top talent can move abroad out of the blue. Your top successor can stop wanting career progression. Your new superstar hire turns out to be unhappy in a new location. A massive and admired brand opens up a contact centre next to yours. The best candidate rejects the job at the last minute. And there is the complexity that makes up all the moving parts that comprise the *resourcing mix*. Permanent staff, contractors, graduates, apprentices, outsourced departments, hourly temporary staff. There may also be the political reality that there are internal vested interests who are happy with things as they are.

And it is all about people and how they *think* and *feel*. People think and feel about work and how they move jobs in complicated ways. They make decisions about career choices, changes and jobs for a myriad of different reasons. Different things influence and motivate at different life stages. New house and new baby—money is king. Financially secure and bored—variety in role. Young and single—working abroad. There are many permutations.

Resourcing is a difficult thing to get right because of these complexities. It's difficult to get right if thoughtfully approached, but almost impossible without a plan. Do you have a plan that gives you the best chance of getting it right? A strategy for resourcing?

This book dismisses the belief that resourcing is a tactical HR operation and promotes the thinking that it is business critical. An immensely underplayed business critical advantage. There is no *five easy steps to the complete resourcing strategy* here, rather a challenge to current ways of thinking and practice.

It is not just about fixing problems. Effective resourcing isn't only about avoiding the disasters, it is about creating opportunities. There is a massive prize to be won. Strategic resourcing will deliver a sustainable and real competitive edge. Your investment in building the capability will be insignificant when compared with the benefit. The challenges with resourcing that your organisation has are precisely those faced by your competitors. They won't have a strategy either. They may be in different locations and they may struggle with different skill sets, but they will also have the weakness and reactionary cycles in the absence of a strategic resourcing approach.

If getting the right people, with the right skills in the right place at the right time, is something that you can do more often and more sustainably than them, your position is strengthened and theirs is weakened. To draw on a sporting analogy, you will be putting your best team out on the pitch in every match. Putting out the best team means you are giving yourself the best possible chance of winning. That's what strategic resourcing is all about. Maximising the probability that you can be at your best more often. Maximising your chances of sustained success.

This book shows you what you need to be thinking about to achieve this. A strategy that will avoid the ambushes. A strategy that will deliver competitive advantage.

Hire Power

CHAPTER 2
THE PLANNING PARADOX

"Measure twice, cut once."

Every carpenter on the planet

We know that business leaders see finding the right skills as a critical problem. Why is that? This pressure is usually put down to skill shortages in the market, changes in the business environment, a failure in the education system or some other external reason. These are all genuine factors, but only if the strategic planning to deal with organisation resourcing has failed to account for them. The lack of strategic resource planning, driven by structure and attitude maintain this status quo. The problem can be resolved, but thinking needs to change.

In HR, particularly resourcing, reacting trumps planning. A thriving recruitment industry is testament to this. The bread and butter of the recruitment industry is the distress purchase. A distress purchase in hiring occurs when a vacancy arises and there isn't a better plan than asking an external agent to find a replacement at a considerable fee. According to the professional body of the recruitment industry, the Recruitment and Employment Confederation, the recruitment industry in the UK has an annual value of £35.1 billion. In recruitment fees generated for permanent recruitment alone, it is worth over £7 billion. This is a substantial industry.

The irony is that a focus on cost for transactional resourcing maintains a tactical reactionary situation which perpetuates a high cost. Not only will a shift in thinking improve the capability and skills in the business, but it will also ultimately reduce the cost of resourcing.

There is a reactivity and an immediacy throughout human resources that is both essential and intensely stifling. HR is first and foremost a service to the business, and reacting quickly to business needs is essential. It is mandated to perform certain essential transactional functions like pay and rations or the administration of joining and leaving. It needs to be reactive to help managers and employees as and when needed, and to build policy frameworks that balance the needs of those employees and the business. It is the function to drive leadership development, performance management, restructures, and of course hiring.

In many industries HR will have a regulatory obligation and in all industries HR will be the internal guardians of many legal responsibilities. There are many things that HR simply has to get done, and many of them require swift action, or at least the business leaders expect quick action. After all, HR is pretty much just sitting there, waiting for the call. Or, so goes much common thinking.

All HR leaders will build strategies to support the business, and the reality of their team being dragged *into the weeds* becomes a tremendous frustration. For a great many HR directors their function becomes almost entirely reactive and strategy is delivered as an afterthought. Moving from one crisis solution to another. Called in to clear up a mess. Largely, because it is a function that is expected to be reactive. Not only because the business leaders expect that when they want something from human resources it will happen immediately, but it is also perpetuated by many of the professionals in the industry itself, who value this responsiveness to the business. In many organisations *responsiveness* is a pseudo-competency, or a core value of the human resources function. This is laudable when you are delivering a service, without doubt. However, there is a very simple human reflex to continue behaving the way that gets rewarded and when the positive feedback from the business is based around reactivity. The impact though, is that many in HR rarely get the opportunity to lift their heads and survey the landscape.

HR AND STRATEGY

HR strategy is directed at many things that are of immense value, in themselves they will contribute to building capability, initiating culture change, mitigating risks or meeting legislative obligations. Training programmes that develop leaders, management development to keep front-line managers consistent in their performance management approach, graduate programmes, health and well-being programmes, diversity approaches. Many of these initiatives will have been introduced as a direct result of feedback from the business and will demonstrate HR's prized responsiveness. Many will be legal or regulatory. They may even link together with a nice strapline or branding. *Back to basics. Good to great. Putting people first.*

This list of HR initiatives is important and of value. All worthy of the resource allocated to them. Do they solve the headaches based in resourcing that the business leadership don't even know are coming? Why is getting the right people still a CEO's biggest headache? Why are 87% of CEOs still bemoaning the inability to get the right skills? Is HR strategy thinking about and pointing at the right things? Where is the focus on resourcing strategically?

No one in HR feels the need for and the pressure to be responsive and reactive more than those with responsibility for resourcing or recruitment. It's a self-perpetuating cycle for recruiters. They are viewed as transactional and tactical service providers. Only important at the point of need, and then critical. So, they tend to react in a highly immediate, transactional and tactical way. Too often there is a hurly-burly freneticism and an excitement in the recruitment team. It is also true that many recruiters love the energy, love the pace of the function and love the definite outcome at the end. After all, it is the only function of HR which can be measured in pure binary terms. You fill the vacancy, or you don't. It's immensely satisfying to solve problems and see the jobs getting filled.

Of course, every head of resourcing will have a strategy. Rather, it is more accurate to say, they have a strategy to fill vacancies. A strategy to meet a tactical objective. There are many people devising plans to address resourcing issues. There will be strong plans for each campaign as they arise, a plan to introduce new applicant tracking technology, a plan to reduce agency expenditure, a plan to change the employer branding, a recruitment strategy for social media, a talent strategy. All of these are important things, but without being linked to the entire resourcing mix, and a long-term horizon, they will merely be better tools to deliver tactically with. Without the awareness that this status quo is an issue, then however good these initiatives are the underlying issues will remain. It's a more efficient status quo.

This is the resourcing *planning paradox*. Caught in the hamster wheel of delivery, viewed as a transactional delivery mechanism for new people and working to role and campaign cycles. With that CEO concern about getting the right skills not disappearing anytime soon, is it not time to think differently about the problem? What is it that stops the development of a plan that has a single focus on delivering the right resource for the business in six months, a year ahead, three years and beyond?

To put it bluntly, HR isn't being challenged to deliver on a strategic, long-term resourcing plan. It is challenged to deliver an annual resourcing plan. There is a narrowness in planning cycles that drives a way of addressing the problems that keep it in the present. A barrier to strategic resource planning is that fundamental. Financial plans work in annual cycles, but people's careers don't. That is a clash of different rhythms, and resource planning is shoehorned into the finance planning process.

FINANCIAL PLANNING

In a standard business planning cycle at the end of the financial year every department submits to finance what they require to meet their objectives for the following year, in terms of budget and headcount. There is generally a bit of back and forth until they agree on a number. A simplified summary, but accurate. Of course, the cycle applies equally to the HR function. For non-income generating functions the back and forth negotiations can be more challenging. It is more difficult to justify additional budget when you are already a cost. This means that there is a reset at the start of each annual cycle when it comes to resourcing. The thinking about developing or hiring a workforce to do the jobs in three years (that may not even exist currently) needs planned for now. A challenge when the most distant horizon is twelve months out at best.

There is a secondary, more immediate problem in the annual planning cycle that restricts the ability for strategic resourcing. In this planning cycle, the recruitment team will base their planned activity on the proposed headcount increase and estimated turnover in all other departments. Given that HR will submit their plan at the same time as everyone else, that becomes an exercise in educated guesswork. In some businesses, where there is scale and known history, this educated guess can be accurate, but for other businesses, or areas within a business it is a repetitive annual headache for HR to negotiate the recruitment budget for the year.

The best-case scenario for HR is to be in a position to recruit to an accurate resource plan for the next year. Hardly a long-term commitment to building the required capability for a long-term plan. The worst case is that HR works with hugely inaccurate numbers and spends a disproportionate amount of time trying to meet a capricious hiring ask. Those are the problems when HR *owns* the budget for the activities that make up the recruitment process. In organisations where the budget for hiring is left with the hiring business area, the chances of hiring being part of a larger strategic plan are greatly reduced.

Company A is a global IT services business. Their view of planning is a great example of how the annual planning cycle restricts the recruitment team's ability to be effective and continually secure the best talent. Their planning cycle is a rigid January to January cycle, with the year's recruitment numbers released at the start of the year for the recruitment department to work on. After planning how to achieve the hiring, and in which locations, the recruitment team essentially has an annual requirement of growth to cram into a five-month window. The result is they don't always secure the best talent, despite their fantastic brand and product range. Due to their ongoing success they don't see resourcing as a strategic enabler, but will this view eventually cause issues? What are they missing out on? What problems do they have that they don't know they have?

The next barrier is the challenge of HR and how it manages resourcing operating in silos. Recruitment, temporary labour decisions, talent movement and internal moves all sit separately, but are all part of the resourcing mix. All present their own issues and all contribute towards the capability map.

TALENT MANAGEMENT

Many large businesses will have a talent function, which helps identify and develop the people in the business who perform best and have potential to go on to greater things. In smaller businesses, the personnel manager will always have *talent* as a key priority. This is important activity. There is clearly a place in organisations for making sure that they know who the best people are and helping them rise as far as their abilities and attitude will take them. However, the risk is that talent sits in a bubble, and whilst the focus may be on building capability, the focus is on building capability of a few individuals without a clear organisational end benefit.

All too frequently the impact is to make a small number of people feel good about themselves and produce a set of reports on the progress of talent, to reduce anxiety showing that the best people are ring-fenced and supported. Are traditional approaches to talent management effective in maintaining the best people and securing a high-performing future? If you ask someone who has been identified as top talent in an organisation, their response to this label is as likely to be, "Yeah...., and?" as opposed to a tale of a structured career path. Of course, they will often have received some great training and development as part of being talent but if there isn't a destination it really is a bit of *so what*? This challenge is faced by many talent professionals—if there aren't the opportunities, then what do you do?

A rather disquieting reality of talent programmes is the strange reality that being on such a thing serves to make that talented individual much more marketable to other employers. It's almost the first thing the agency recruitment consultant or headhunter will put on a candidate summary. If an experienced interviewer has heard once in an interview from the candidate that they are considered top talent and are on the fast track, they'll have heard it a thousand times. And it works. It's just human nature to find that level of external validation an attractive endorsement. It's particularly attractive if the interviewer themself was once in a talent pool, and can relate to the *brilliance* that it takes to be recognised as such. Given that most senior executives will have been considered talent at some stage in their careers, the appeal is obvious.

Company B is a sizable financial service firm. A senior legal counsel there was considered top talent. On the succession plan, she was the named successor for the next level up, which happened to be the only legal director-level position. The incumbent director was also talent and decided to move laterally within the firm as part of career progression, leaving the vacancy. Of course, the succession plan kicked into place.

Not quite. There was a humming and hawing as to whether she was quite ready for the promotion, and a decision was made to look to the market. To see what was *out there*.

The expectation was still that she would be appointed, but you never know what would come along in a search. The hesitation and lack of confidence was evident to her, and a headhunter called her at a serendipitous moment for them both to talk about a bigger job with a competitor.

She went for the interview, of course, for the much more senior position. In the interview, she naturally highlighted the fact that she was the successor and considered to be top talent. She was convinced that this made all the difference when measured against competition of equal technical ability.

Her new employers were impressed, and she got the offer. An offer which outstripped her expectations, and removed any lingering thoughts of staying on. The decision was met with considerable dismay at her former firm, who berated themselves for losing someone on the talent and succession list.

INTERNAL MOBILITY

Internal mobility (people moving from role to role in the same organisation) is more often than not a manifestation of company culture rather than a planned way of getting resources in the right place. This is simply people moving about the organisation by applying for jobs without wanting to leave the organisation, but wanting a new role, or a more senior role.

Two of the UK's top banks are very similar organisations, but the culture of internal mobility is starkly different. Both organisations have had difficult days, but both are full of really bright people doing interesting things. They are very similar in structure and products, scale and international reach. Analysis in Bank A showed that some 75% of the mid-level jobs were filled internally and the rest were filled from the external market. In Bank B, the position was virtually the reverse.

There are a few reasons for such a significant gap. One was headquartered in London and one in Edinburgh. Bank A had a more technically advanced level of internal job board integration between divisions. Bank B operated with a more federated divisional structure. However, the fundamental cultural difference was that for most Bank A managers the first thought for a vacancy was for someone inside and in Bank B the case was to look outside if there was nothing in the immediate department. It would be an easy assumption to make to say that Bank A had it right and Bank B needs to work on it, but that's only the case if the internal movement in Bank A was meeting their capability requirements. In both organisations, it just happened that way. Yes, Bank A wanted a healthy internal job market, but it wasn't designed as such in a way to align to any notion of a strategic resourcing approach. It was a culture that was encouraged and welcomed, but wasn't designed.

Many internal moves are simply people moving about a department. The manager has a gap in one part, and opens it up to the rest of the team, who apply and someone moves. It's good for the team, good for the manager and creates an environment where career advancement is visible and positive. All good. Good if that's what you want to create. If you want to create an environment in which people across the business become multiskilled this approach will restrict that intra-departmental movement. It's not that one is right and that one is wrong. It simply isn't considered to be part of an overall resourcing plan, it is accidental rather than part of a longer-term strategy to push business performance.

TEMPORARY LABOUR

Another part of the resourcing mix that has variable degrees of planning is that of temporary labour. In many industries, temporary or contract staff are a valuable, often critical resource. Hotel chains would struggle without seasonal temps, Christmas food shopping in your local supermarket would be chaos without them, and the farming industry has a massive reliance on casual and temporary labour. Contractor staff are the engine behind just about any IT or engineering project across the globe. Sick cover, maternity leave, sabbatical cover, all perfectly good reasons for using temporary labour. A planned and appropriate level of temporary workers is an essential part of a huge number of businesses.

The problem comes when the level isn't planned, or a temporary employee is hired for a permanent role. There isn't a finite defined project end point, no one is returning to the role and there are no plans to remove the role. It's a permanent position. As well as the service impact, there can be other issues. At Four Seasons, the cost of the temporary labour force has been critical, for other organisations it may be that too much of the intellectual capital sits with people who have no long-term allegiance to the organisation. There is also the cost aspect of employing temporary staff. So, there are lots of very compelling reasons to restrict the use of temporary staff to occasions of positive design rather than when it presents a risk.

However, organisations will often slide into the use of temporary or contract staff for reasons that aren't positive design. The most common is an inability to secure permanent resource for those roles. In many technical IT positions, there is market pressure in that the skills for certain specialisms just don't exist as permanent employee resource, and can only be found in contractors. In high turnover environments, like contact centres, or warehouses, temporary labour is often the quickest way of backfilling. It is also the case that temporary labour is the resourcing route of choice in many such environments, because they don't trust their ability to attract and assess suitable staff on a permanent basis, so justify the reliance on temporary hiring as a *try-before-you-buy* strategy.

Then there is inertia: when temporary staff are hired who then seem to be doing a good job and the manager continually extends the contract to keep them around. With technical skills the day-rate temporary contractor can make a very healthy living dotting about from department to department. This is easy recruitment. Reliable, skilled workers providing a key skill and already on-site. There are many reasons, intended and unintended why organisations use contract and temporary staff. This is a significant part of the resourcing mix.

At the centre of the misallocation of temporary labour, is that problem with planning, again. The lack of a plan, the lack of a strategic outlook for resourcing. The use of temporary staff is so often a reaction to an event that wasn't planned for, or the planning didn't look at the right thing.

This illustrates many institutional and cultural problems that stop strategic resourcing from taking place. There is the idea that the problem isn't acknowledged as being a strategic one. The lack of available skills issue is treated tactically. There are the HR strategies that cover a vast array of competing agendas, that all impact overall capability, but operate in silos. Then there is the short-term approach that exists in the planning that does happen. Within each strand of the resourcing mix, there are flaws in planning and issues created by non-planning, that keep the operators in those silos constantly fighting fires. The use of recruitment is tactical, temporary labour is tactical, internal mobility is tactical, talent is separate and business leadership doesn't ask HR to examine the fundamental challenge—the resourcing mix of the future.

Chris had been at Lothian Bank for a number of years and loved her job as HR director. She came through the HR graduate programme of one of the top high street banks and had a reputation in Lothian as being a real go-getter. No nonsense, straight talking.

She found James great to work with, although sometimes she felt he didn't quite see the strategic value in HR. However, he ensured that Chris sat as part of the executive team and they had regular one-to-ones. She considered the working relationship to be very strong, moreover she liked James and believed that his strong value set was a great bedrock for his leadership. She knew that he trusted her, as he would frequently talk about the issues he was facing.

That trust helped with his complete endorsement of her *people plan*, and the way she structured the HR team. She structured HR in a typical HR business partner (HRBP) model, with a central team of deep specialists for training, policy, resourcing and talent. There is the all-important administration team for pay, rations and admin and a small change team to drive the strategic change agenda.

The people plan was her core road map of activity for the next year and it had a couple of main themes.

Management capability at front-line level operations. There was a significant learning and development initiative to support this, with classroom and online training modules. The other key element was a focus on leadership capability for the top 150 in the business, aligned to the business values. Of course, there are all the other essentials—keeping the show on the road, building the graduate programme, developing the manager advice line, cycle to work scheme, pension changes and a new reward strategy for technical staff (a response to the challenges in recent IT growth). Not to mention the diversity strategy she was passionate about. She trusted her team to deliver their bits of the plan, so she was able to focus on managing the relationships with the executive.

She mulled over the last meeting she had with James. He was agitated. Little things were going wrong and he was developing a concern about the overall capability of the bank. Capability concerns that he felt would stop the growth plans if left unresolved. He was frustrated that he couldn't see or articulate a clear solution.

The issues were a cocktail of different things: growing regret at a recent hire he had made, frustration at the expansion of his senior team, fears about IT security and the dipping customer service levels. Chris had listened and offered support in the areas where she might be able to help.

She volunteered Lucy to do a review of the temporary staff in the contact centre. She said that her head of talent, would work with the director of mortgages to uncover what development areas there were. They both agreed on that, but they both quietly thought that he wasn't the great choice they thought he was, and if he survived the next few months, it only be then that they would they see if he was big enough for the role.

On the matter of the frustrations with the building and expansion of the executive team, Chris had left the meeting feeling that she and her department should really have been closer to that. No point in regretting it now, but a lesson for the future. The exercise to identify successors was part of the annual talent cycle. She was pleased that Simon had a process for talent mapping through the entire management structure of the organisation. They knew who were the high performers with great potential, and theoretically then who should be in line for the next big jobs. They had undertaken an exercise to identify all the success for director and executive positions and on paper that had gone very well. Some gaps, but that was to be expected, but otherwise a named successor for every senior position in the bank. On paper. And it ticked a box with the regulator, who liked to ask about these things.

However, when push came to shove, that plan on paper turned out to be just a *plan on paper*. No translation into real activity. James was particularly frustrated with the problem of building the senior team, as it was the thing that most directly impacted him, and it's what he saw as critical. Chris was mindful of the notion that in some way he would and should be frustrated with her about that problem. After all her team owned the process. She frowned with the realisation that they had done what was asked, completed the exercise and possibly hadn't kicked the tyres quite enough. Nor had she when she looked at the final plans and raised her eyebrows at a few of the names identified as ready for next role. People who clearly weren't, but it was a name in a box. A paper exercise indeed.

She was relieved that the cybersecurity threat concern was eased by the great work of Lucy and her team in driving the recruitment through in a really short time. She recalled the tension at that point and Lucy's justified annoyance at the demand for scarce skills with so little notice. It was like no one saw this coming. At the same time, she knew that Lucy was pretty much facing the same thing again from IT, with their new online team expansion and digital projects. It wasn't that the IT team didn't know what direction they were going, and it wasn't that they didn't work well with the recruitment team, but it was just now a frequent problem. She always got great feedback about the recruitment team from the IT director, as he always voiced that there was a real partnership in the thick of the action when recruiting. It was always just a little bit too much of all hands to the pump recruitment, and frantic activity.

It dawned on her that what they were doing wasn't good enough. They had focused on delivering initiatives that were right at the time, but were all just sticking plasters. Of course, she had always focused on capability, and efforts to raise the bar with managers and staff, but it was always just reactionary. A response to issues, or when it was demanded at an executive meeting. They just spent too much time in the weeds.

They were now facing a potential capability crisis, if James's anxiety was well founded. Perhaps the crisis was already upon them. That was a sobering thought. She had never really challenged herself, or the executive, if they were doing the right things to ensure long-term capability. The capability they required to fulfil their ambitions.

She started to see a way of approaching the problem and knew the very person in her team to drive it with her. Fortunately, they were due to meet later that day.

Lucy was preparing for her meeting with Chris. She had specifically requested to meet because she desired to change the way things are done in recruitment and she could only make it happen with Chris's full support and sponsorship. She had kept her fully apprised of her concerns about how the function operated, but that didn't stop her feeling nervous as she thought about asking for changes she wanted to make.

For a start, she would be asking Chris to campaign to have the recruitment budget completely centralised, and that was definitely going to be a battle. As it stood the head of resourcing held the budget for volume recruitment and the candidate and campus attraction budget for the small graduate programme they ran, but head office recruitment budgets were held by each individual business area. Recruitment agencies loved Lothian Bank. Head office budget centralisation was just a start.

In her short time with the business Lucy had already written her shopping list of things to change, which she grouped under three headings. Capability, governance and technology. It was kinder to put the list of ailments in the three buckets, rather than a single bucket–*everything*. After all Chris had been in charge of HR for some time, and Lucy didn't want to criticise everything that had gone before.

Chris liked what Lucy said, and her way of thinking. That was why she knew that Lucy was the ideal person to come with her to meet with James to outline the plan she was formulating. When they met, she listened to Lucy's suggestions, and told her that was the starting point. They were going to do something much bigger, and something that was critical.

There was a lot of work ahead of them to even understand what the issues and barriers were, before making a plan. It was going to be very difficult. Chris relished the prospect that they had the opportunity to make a lasting difference. Lucy wondered just what she had let herself in for.

Hire Power

CHAPTER 3
DISCOVERY

"There are known knowns; there are things we know we know. We also know there are known unknowns; that is to say we know there are some things we do not know. But there are also unknown unknowns—the ones we don't know we don't know"

Donald Rumsfeld, US Secretary for Defense

Lucy emerged from the meeting with Chris with a slight sense of panic. She hadn't been with the business long, but she had been there long enough. Long enough to carry the can for the things that were going wrong. She already knew some of the issues that she had wanted to address with Chris, but the request now was for a deep dive. She suspected that she would find a great many things she didn't particularly like. Ultimately, as she was well aware, she was accountable for all recruitment issues. Not only was she accountable but she would stand in front of the Chief Exec and tell him exactly what the problems were. "Warts and all," Chris had said, "leave nothing out. This could be our only chance to effect real change. No stone unturned."

There had been a real drive in the tone Chris had taken in the meeting and she firmly stated the need for a shared common objective to put any personal or team agendas to one side. She was definitely on a mission. They were going to get to the bottom of what was causing the issues that all came back to recruitment or talent. Simply put, what were the reasons they didn't have the right people, in the right place at the right time?

Back at her desk as her mind raced, Lucy figured out the only way to approach the problem was to break it down. "Eat the elephant one chunk at a time," a former boss would patronisingly say. Attract, assess, onboard. However, she knew they weren't quite the chunks she needed. There were larger, more strategic problems. Or lack of a strategy, more like.

As she was fresh in, Lucy had already cast a critical eye over the department she had inherited. A review with the intention to take recommendations to Chris and work on a programme of continuous improvement. Was this now going to be revolution, not evolution? The early impressions were enough for her to fear what the rest would tell her, and she suspected that ugly things would crawl out from under the stones she was about to turn over. That concerned her and, new as she was, it was unavoidable that the bad news would probably stick to her. She didn't particularly relish exposing her fledgling career at Lothian Bank to the *blame game*.

Lucy quickly came to the decision as to how she would tackle the exercise. Start with the more strategic themes and work downwards to the detail. In her mind, the strategic parts of the recruitment cycle were planning, employer branding, and how things were delivered—the operating model. Then she would probe deeper into the component parts of that process, candidate generation, assessment, offer and onboarding. She wanted to understand what everyone did, what the process was, what technology was used and just how effective the whole lot was when thrown together.

Lucy knew they had a recruitment policy. It talked about the concepts of fairness, the need to use bank tools in assessment, the need to adhere to branding guidelines. What it didn't do was define any level of roles and responsibilities in the process. What she didn't know was if the practice resembled the policy, and who was doing what.

What bothered her more than her own plight, was the concern she had that the recruitment practices and structure might be doing some *damage*. Not once in the first few weeks had she seen or heard anything that was definitively focused on improving the quality of hiring. Furthermore, she had heard precious little talk about candidates, but lots of talk in the team of filling jobs quickly. In the balance of time, cost and quality in hiring, Lucy was all too aware that a focus on one would have a negative impact on another. She feared the time pressure was a factor in hurting quality hiring.

Her own experience in joining revealed a candidate experience that was just about passable. However, she had been a successful applicant, and she suspected that it was much poorer for the declined candidates. Just how many of them went on to describe their experiences to their friends? Just how many never considered Lothian for their banking? In head office, the pools of candidates they recruited from were small and often in the same network. Just what level of damage had been done to any future recruitment? She knew that the lack of partnership between the recruitment team and the experts in the technical areas was a problem. This lack of internal coordination could be having a detrimental external branding impact.

She knew that recruitment sat too far downstream in the planning process. They always received capacity planning information very late and even then, it was messy or imprecise, or non-existent in places. There was nothing that resembled workforce planning. There were headcount numbers and manpower targets. Mostly meaningless, mostly subject to change, and change they did. Not only did this reveal a failing in planning processes, it spoke volumes about how recruitment was viewed. They were always going to struggle to deliver effectively if they weren't getting good plans to work to.

Employer branding was an issue that Lucy had spotted on day one. Indeed, she had spotted it before day one. Being in the business of recruitment, Lucy had analysed her own experience, and looked at a range of Lothian Bank's online job advertisements and had seen massive inconsistencies in approach. She wasn't sure if Lothian had an approach to managing their employer brand. Even just considering that there wasn't one pretty much reinforced in her mind that they probably didn't.

More than that, she spoke to agencies she'd worked with before and asked them how they promoted Lothian Bank. All variations on a theme, but the theme certainly wasn't the official Lothian Bank line. Finally, she had spoken to a couple of friends who worked there before making a final decision to join, and they smiled when Lucy showed them what the employer branding message was. "I think that's what they'd like to be," was the response.

The third strategic point for Lucy was the operating model that recruitment had for the business. Quite simply how did they work with line managers and candidates to get a result? Did they have a *white-glove-do-everything-hand-holding* model? Did they leave it all up to the line managers? Did they vary the delivery approach by level? By salary? By area? By geography? By business? In her short time there, Lucy hadn't quite got to the bottom of the operating model.

Possibly because no one called it the operating model. Her recruitment managers had looked at her rather blankly and Lucy got the idea that they all did some recruitment *stuff*. Oh dear. Clarity of role was important to Lucy. Made things easier. *Stuff* made things messy.

After digging up a lack of anything she could reliably call strategic, Lucy strongly suspected that what lay underneath would be a continuation on a theme. The lack of direction, planning and proposition definition would certainly mean constant tactical firefighting. How did they generate candidates for their vacancies, assess them and what was the detail in the candidate experience?

The attraction of applications to Lothian Bank was heavily reliant on recruitment agencies. Part of the challenge that Chris had given her when she started was to bring that down. She was given a cost-saving target. Lucy saw a future where Lothian did its own recruitment, rather than using lots of high cost agencies. She was also troubled that any other advertising that was already being done by the team just didn't seem terribly effective. Perhaps that contributed to the use of agencies?

Lucy knew little of the assessment practices used in the business, but she also knew that reporting back on assessment was critical, and would be an area of interest for Chris and James. Her expectations were low. Later, she would find that these low expectations were unrealistically high.

Lucy would also look at the offer and onboarding process. Lucy's own onboarding (into HR for goodness sake!) had been disappointing. A week without a phone and two days when she couldn't log in. Not a disaster, but...

Mulling over all the pieces and reflecting on her own experience in applying to and joining Lothian, Lucy knew there was much that just didn't work well. It didn't work well in the component parts and it certainly didn't join up well. That was part of the attraction for Lucy, ironically enough. She knew that this recruitment process was in her gift to fix, and that was a great opportunity, a real challenge. It appealed to her, because she was passionate about delivering a great candidate experience. At the very least, centring the Lothian Bank recruitment focus on that one thing was going to make a massive difference.

She knew things were broken, and that was what she would have to say. The detail would reveal how badly and where. On the upside though, she knew she had Chris's support and that she was definitely receptive to hearing thoughts on improvements. What made her feel a little queasy was that she would have to share such a poor picture with the CEO so soon. A CEO who seemed reasonable, but her only encounter with him was a brief introduction. How would he react to a mess, if that's what things were? Did he know she was new? Would he just outsource the problem? Bring in management consultants to recommend changes? None of these were prospects Lucy relished at all. However, her resolve was to just go after the issues and tell it as it was. Nothing else for it.

CHAPTER 4
SELF-AWARENESS

"Honesty is the first chapter in the book of wisdom."

Thomas Jefferson

The next few months were a time of discovery for Lucy. She completed the review with urgency, precision and no small amount of anxiety, eye-rolling and, at times, total horror. She came to terms with the fact that there was going to be little good to report back on, and as she proceeded through the exercise, nothing changed her thinking.

The report could be presented to say that there was no terminal failure with recruitment. It could say the function operated to a level of expectation. Targets were largely hit, and it was consistently under budget. There was a recruitment policy in place. They had a careers website and used applicant tracking technology. There was a regular stream of new joiners.

Whilst there was delivery and nothing was obviously critically broken, underneath the surface the practice, handovers, uncertainties, inefficiencies and inconsistencies led to an unfortunate conclusion. The recruitment team did not contribute *anything* to improving quality.

They were, however, good at ensuring warm bodies were in place. Furthermore, the drivers, measures and capability of hiring managers often actively worked against any notion that they could guarantee the level of capability required. A deeply uncomfortable conclusion.

Lucy wanted to start with the employer branding work that had been done, or if an employee value proposition (EVP) had been developed. One that presented a positive image of the bank, but at the same time accurately refelected the working experience there. Like most places the bank had its good points and its bad points.

With its modest scale, every role in the bank had much more scope and responsibility than at a similar level in a larger bank, where people tended to be more siloed. That was a great selling point for many people—a real chance to develop their skills and grow in a job. The flip side was that it was a pretty high-pressure organisation as it had grown quickly and people had to deliver in short timescales. The small size meant that people had that extra responsibility, it also meant that performance was visible at senior level for many roles. It wasn't for everyone.

The previous Lothian Bank head of resourcing had commissioned some EVP work from a major advertising communications company, but as Lucy went through their final presentation and recommendation she realised it fell well short of the mark. It simply didn't tell the positive aspects of the story, or suggest what the reality was to people who might not thrive with such visibility.

The only significant thing it achieved, in what turned out to be a rather expensive PowerPoint presentation, was to play back the bank *values* and the staff commitments that Chris and the team had developed years before around teamwork, honesty and openness. The results were beautifully presented. These weren't bad sentiments, and the bank values of integrity, customer service and innovation were equally noble. However, it wasn't really telling a story that staff recognised or which informed candidates. Nor did it sell anything unique about the organisation.

The EVP work looked like a piece of work by a supplier that they knew would land perfectly with the executive, which it did, by telling them pretty much what they wanted to hear. There was an advertising style and internal communication devices were produced off the back of it, but frankly they could have represented working anywhere, with a laudable, but anodyne set of corporate values. Lucy knew that this was not getting the right message to the right people. Uncomfortable finding number one.

THE EMPLOYER BRAND

Having an employer brand and an associated EVP that can be easily articulated is a critical part of recruitment activity. The industry behind employer branding may be laden with jargon and buzzwords, but the underlying concepts are cornerstone principles of successful resourcing.

The employer brand is what anyone (employees, potential candidates, customers or any person who holds a view of your business) thinks about what it's like to work in your business. On the back of the brand, the EVP is the sales proposition. What are the most appealing things about working for your organisation and how do you tell people?

Utilising your employer brand successfully is an exercise in understanding and communicating a positive perspective of what it means to work in your organisation. A perspective that is founded on the reality.

Most organisations of any size will now undertake some employer branding work, to understand what the world thinks of them as employers and then attempt to manipulate that message. Some will attempt to craft an image of themselves that is unrecognisable. Unrecognisable to candidates, and worse still, staff. This is an expensive and futile exercise if used to mask an unpleasant working environment. Staff won't buy the deception and candidates will either be better informed, or find out the reality at some stage.

Through research, social media, the internet, their friends or the media, candidates have a firm idea what a company is like before they make an application, even before they even see any of your advertising. There are many factors that influence how a potential future employee will view a business and optimistic words in an advertisement are unlikely to shift fixed attitudes. A poor employer brand will impact the number of applicants. It will also have a significant impact on the calibre of candidates. Good people always have choices.

The trap that Lothian Bank fell into, having an EVP presentation that played back words they had already written, is not an outlandish one. Bank A is one of the UK's largest and most well-known companies, a full-service international bank, and they commissioned extensive and expensive EVP work.

The work and output was enthusiastically received, but subsequently only yielded a fraction of return on that investment by way of change to some genuine resourcing problems. Bank A had recently redefined the corporate values, and the presentation was simply an overt playback of the new words, with hefty research to demonstrate why they resonated with people and how they could be communicated. What it didn't do was reflect what life was like in the organisation, it just communicated an executive aspiration of environment and behaviour.

This was an organisation with a high early turnover issue with the technical and management populations, a key reason was a mismatch between external perception and the reality of working there. The EVP work did nothing to address this, but the output looked fantastic. The presentation was very popular with the executive and HR leadership, but it didn't really tackle the difficult truths. The market perception was—*takes its pound of flesh, pays great.*

That would be an honest starting point. A starting point to build the narrative to reach the executive aspiration, but the work avoided the challenging realities. It was significantly easier to tell people what they wanted to hear.

Great case study for the supplier, though. Not to mention a decent payday.

The value of any exercise to understand the employer brand is an exercise in self-awareness. You will not want to shout the downsides from the rafters, but you need to be aware of them, so they can be managed through the process. The only way of dealing with the poor aspects of a brand is to recognise them.

CAPACITY PLANNING

Following the EVP analysis, Lucy turned her attention to the planning process, starting with capacity planning for the contact centres. This was not *owned* by her team, but rather by the various operations teams who coordinated operations resource planning and the feed to the recruitment team for the required demand. They converted the marketing data into the call time required and how many people they would need to answer the phones, how many desks they would need and what recruitment was required. They also considered the anticipated turnover in the contact centres, and growth plans.

The problem for the recruitment team was that the amount of hiring that they were predicted to manage over the course of the year only bore a passing resemblance to what they actually ended up doing. The number that was projected and ultimately hired could be close, but the phasing of when those people were required was always way out. As she reviewed the previous few years' projections, an initial plan for 100 in any given month, could become 150 when the requisition to start the hiring was submitted, then be reduced to 120 and then they would hire 160, with 80 of them being temporary staff.

This caused huge frustration in the volume recruitment team as they had to plan against constantly shifting numbers. It created immense advertising, candidate management and logistical problems for them, and meant they were always playing catch-up. They had always intended to develop talent pools of quality candidates to speed up recruitment, but the constantly shifting sands kept this an unrealised intention.

The lack of accurate data was also a major problem for the resource planning team. Firstly, they themselves received vague information about what the call volume would be based on product marketing drives. They also often fell victim to unplanned incidents that drove up the level of calls received when there were errors or problems. They often struggled to identify the average length of call as products changed, which made planning headcount impossible. They wanted to give the recruitment team accurate and timely data (after all, it was to their benefit), but sometimes it just wasn't possible. Everybody found this situation a constant irritant, but no one seemed the have the time or the imagination to solve it.

Lucy's look at capacity planning for head office and IT roles revealed a picture she was already aware of. There wasn't any, but there were headcount targets for each department, and they recruited as and when a manager had the authority to expand, or needed a replacement. Her team was aware of the numbers for each department, but since they didn't hold the budget for head office recruitment, they were entirely reactionary to the needs as they arose.

What Lucy realised from day one, was that this meant that almost the only thought process for recruitment was to use recruitment agencies, leaving no budget for long-term process or branding initiatives. Addressing this had been high on her to-do list but she faced resistance from every head office team who would be handing budget over to her. They liked the control, and in any case, didn't see a problem.

All in all, Lucy's diagnosis was precisely as she had suspected all along. Capacity planning, resource planning and simple accuracy of the numbers her team worked with were as good as useless. This created problems throughout the hiring process.

Before even getting to the notion that there is a strategic workforce and capability plan to work to, most recruitment teams' problems with planning are often simple tactical issues of certainty about the numbers they will be required to deliver in the short term. Or they frequently deal with demands with short timescales for delivery. There is a simple connection here in that the lack of a strategic plan creates the environment of immediacy and short-term planning that creates the issues. The horizon is too near for real planning, and the recruitment team keeps running around the hamster wheel of delivery.

The issue of changeable targets is a commonplace problem faced by all of those dealing with high-volume, fast-moving environments—where the challenge is to repeatedly recruit many of the same roles on a regular basis. Contact centres, production lines, warehouses, retail staff, etc. The planning challenge for recruitment is that too often they are the final recipients of the planning data, meaning they must act quickly. That puts a focus on numbers and time, rather than quality. Add on the constant focus on the cost per hire target and the emphasis on recruiting quality can be further diminished.

Where the hiring is for fewer, often unique, positions, the planning conundrum is entirely different. On a large scale, the assumptions on turnover and growth are valid, so the overall recruitment numbers for a head office environment is not a difficult number to establish. However, without an extraordinarily detailed view of the motivation of every single individual and when they will leave, each role becomes an individual project. Each project then requires an individual plan.

There are further time pressures. Modern organisations rarely have any roles they can easily carry as vacant for any length of time. When recruitment is driven by a replacement need, the pressure is on from the minute of resignation.

The notice period of the leaver and the recruitment period for the new joiner will not match. The leaver probably has a month's notice. The new joiner will probably also have a month's notice period from their current position. All the time spent finding candidates, assessing candidates, offering, etc., is additional time that the role is unfilled. This very scenario builds pressure into the recruitment process, and this exerts a very simple pressure on quality.

The pressure to fill the role has an impact on quality that may seem subtle, but can be significant. It nurtures a tendency to want the candidates to perform well, so that the recruitment can be completed. This diminishes the prospect of a 100% objective view.

Wanting candidates to perform well at assessment simply steers an assessor's thinking towards seeing the good evidence more vividly and concerns less clearly. As such, there is the chance this positive sentiment, encouraged by a ticking clock, leans towards making a decision that will tend to fill the gap quickly, rather than correctly.

This won't always be the case and is entirely understandable, but this is when you can see people start to make unplanned compromises. Compromises with consequences. Scale that up across a whole business and you start to see an issue that no one even knows exists. Rushed recruitment creates a compromise on capability.

Sometimes the solution to the problem can be as damaging as the problem itself. Company B is an international business services provider and they believed they had measures in place to manage the planning conundrum.

They produced an annual manpower plan, which went through the management team and the appropriate finance governance. It produced, by the end of November, a full plan for the following year. This identified every new role that each department was going to need.

The gaps could be given to the recruitment team in November for them to use as a definitive signed-off recruitment plan. This completely negated the need for any vacancy authorisation and was designed to give the recruitment team a head start and enable them to focus on hiring quality.

All good. However, the fatal flaw in the plan was that as the budget for each role started on January 1 that was precisely when every hiring manager wanted their new headcount to start. Right from the distribution of the plan the recruitment team was up against it.

They had an avalanche of vacancies to plough through in the first quarter, a number of leftovers and new vacancies caused by turnover in the second quarter, a manageable workload for quarter three and an easy end to the year.

Apart from the clear issue that this meant the resource in the recruitment team wasn't ever being used at an optimal level, it also hindered the drive for quality. In quarter one when the bulk of hiring took place the team was so flat out, they just wanted each job off their desk to concentrate on the next. The team had great intentions, but the reality was that a *maybe* was much more likely to become a *yes* rather than a *no*.

If a manager really wanted the best support from the recruitment team, and by extension, the best chance of the best new hire, best wait until quarter four. But who can wait?

Isn't capricious manpower planning just the way it is? Isn't this just something we have to accept and understand that the consequences will always be something we have to put up with? Not at all. The fundamental issues won't change. Planning in a complex environment will always produce margins of error, but the answer to the problem is not to continue trying to fix the planning problem. The answer lies with developing resourcing strategies with an understanding of the limits of the planning problems.

There are sectors and industries where stability and predictability give them an ability to make good solid projections of recruitment numbers. Where the scale is large, turnover is manageable and consistent, the business process and capacity required are well understood and growth is either non-existent or well-planned. For the rest of the world, however, the simple fact is that there are often just too many moving parts to ever command the accuracy we would like, so there is little sense in fretting about the accuracy of planning. It makes much better sense to learn to work effectively with predictions that are going to be unreliable. You can still maximise your chances of making the best hires. It's just a different problem.

One thing Lucy knew she would have to fix as a priority was the recruitment operating model. The vague set of engagement rules whereby her team did *recruitment stuff* for the business. Different *stuff* for different parts of the business, and *stuff* that didn't always add value. However, her team did *stuff* because they always did, or the managers expected it, or because it was administrative, or because the process was just inefficient.

Hiring managers did not have a consistent view of what HR did for them in recruitment. Multiple levels of service had evolved for different parts of the business. Variations in proposition for different areas or levels of seniority wasn't a bad thing, but they had developed through chance rather than design.

Separately, the company intranet had a section outlining the policy and the process, but Lucy suspected that these were just words on the intranet. Nobody ever referenced it. The recruitment team had grown to work with different parts of the business in different ways, and the process and who owned what was a set of unwritten agreements.

The recruitment process workflow was managed on the company's applicant tracking system (ATS). Lothian Bank had recently purchased the world's most popular such system. It was the key deliverable of Lucy's predecessor, and she had chosen the safe option. Examination of how the system was used confirmed Lucy's fears. Even within the recruitment team, use of the system was inconsistent. Some of the team even had their own spreadsheet candidate-management processes they used instead of the ATS, which they would update as an afterthought.

Worse still, after they opened it up to the managers in the business as part of the *manager self-service drive* of the year before, the overall effectiveness of the system declined. The quality of the system management reporting of activity was so inaccurate as to be meaningless. In fact, basic accurate data was impossible to get from the system—open vacancies, ratio of internal against external hiring, time to hire, and so on. Everything that was measured was done so manually, separately, and slightly differently for each manager. Their stakeholders had slightly different expectations, so asked for different types of reports. Being obliging and customer focused, the recruitment team would spend an age pulling together bespoke reports.

Given that the recruitment team was constantly being stretched and there were always recruitment issues emerging that they had no heads-up about, many business areas demanded greater and more frequent reporting to attempt to understand the issues. It was a massive drain on time and was of dubious value.

Lucy looked a little deeper with a series of team and stakeholder interviews to see what people thought of the process. The head office recruitment team aired some old gripes about the hiring mangers they dealt with. They sent the role profile late, it was inaccurate, they just wanted to use agencies but wouldn't attend the agency briefings, they would expect all the administration done, they wouldn't respond to CVs, never gave feedback to declined candidates and always offered too much.

The top frustration for the recruitment team was the idea, fixed in the minds of their internal customers, that the agencies could find someone quicker—someone who was *on their books*. The recruitment managers knew the agencies found most of their candidates on LinkedIn and they also scoured that source for potential candidates. It was frustrating to know that they were simply in a race against the agencies. Many of the agencies had been briefed before the internal recruiter. In fact, it was common practice for the hiring manager to brief their favoured agency before the job was even posted internally, to make sure candidates were lined up. Her team loved their jobs and enjoyed delivering for the managers, but were frustrated that they couldn't do more.

Lucy wanted to know what the hiring managers thought too. Again, she was not surprised by their comments. They were also frustrated. They didn't think that the recruitment team could find good people quickly enough, and that the agencies knew them really well and could find the right candidates quickly. They also had little or no confidence that they would ever find anyone internally. Just a waste of time to advertise on the intranet.

They viewed the recruitment team as essential to get the back-end paperwork done, but felt it slightly got in the way when it came to finding people. They should just stand aside and let the agencies do their work, was the common view. When they did follow the recommended process of posting internally before the recruitment team posted the job online, they reported that they were sent too many CVs. They were irritated that these were often completely inappropriate candidates and it was all a waste of their time. They did often say that they liked the recruitment team. After all, who else would do the administration?

Lucy got additional insight in talking to some recent Lothian Bank joiners. It was well known in the organisations that they came from that if you wanted to get into Lothian Bank the best way was through a few recruitment agencies, as direct applications got ignored. This was what most of them had done, both for head office and contact centre roles. They were delighted that recruitment consultants they went to helped them through the process with the hiring manager, and were even able to give them the heads-up on some of the questions they would be asked in the interview. Lucy was not surprised that the candidates would be vigorously coached through the process, but she was dismayed. It was another blow to the drive for quality hiring.

The few starters who had been recruited by applying directly to the bank spoke of duplication in the application process, inputting data that was already on their CV, delays in communication, being contacted by different people through the process, cancelled interviews, and an overall lack of knowledge of what was going on.

Lucy also spoke to many of the recruitment agency suppliers for head office. The recruitment agency senior management that Lucy spoke to had differing views of working with Lothian Bank. The suppliers on the preferred supplier list (PSL) were frustrated that they had cut their rates to be on a list, yet it was open season for everyone else. The others she spoke to said that they had great relationships with the managers, understood the business, and frankly should be on the PSL. They all complained about slow feedback on CVs and felt the recruitment team just *got in the way*.

Things were also not working well with the internal jobs market. Lucy spoke to some staff who had applied for roles through intranet advertising and, as a result, had moved department. They all expressed the same sentiment at being appointed. Surprise. The belief was that it was difficult to move internally because management would either move people about their own team, or bring in someone they used to work with. Lothian Bank was full of cliques who had worked together in larger organisations beforehand, and looked after each other now.

Not one could say that, even when appointed, they got constructive feedback from the interview. No one had ever heard of anyone getting feedback when they were unsuccessful in their application.

Lucy reviewed her findings with dismay. She realised there was so much tension and dysfunction under the surface that it was virtually broken. It gave her a growing sense of despair. The head office recruitment team and the hiring managers came from completely different perspectives. Some recruitment agencies thrived in this environment, especially those who worked hard at bypassing the process. Those who played by the rules, joined the PSL and kept the recruitment team informed, did less well. Lucy wondered how long it would be before they either drifted off and promoted their best candidates elsewhere, or also bypassed the HR process.

The operating model was different for the high-volume areas—contact centres and branch network. There the recruitment team ran the attraction budget, and managed the candidate logistics. However, even though the operating model and delivery was different, the tensions were very similar.

The volume recruitment team was most frustrated by the planning process. They seemed to get the demand to recruit for large numbers in what they considered to be ridiculous timescales. Timescales and demands that would change. Lucy was already very aware of that issue. They also constantly struggled to get the team leaders to agree to assist in the assessment centre events.

They were constantly going at 100 miles an hour and felt that they weren't appreciated. They felt blamed for everything that went wrong, but were working flat out in difficult circumstances. It was a team under real pressure.

The team managers from the contact centre were equally frustrated. They were already flat out in their day job, and didn't have the time to dedicate to the assessment centres. They found it infuriating when they hung about all day to see *rubbish* candidates. They didn't understand why they couldn't just do an interview. After all, they knew what they wanted.

Many of them just wanted to use a local supplier to bypass recruitment, but didn't have the budget. They got around this by bringing in temps and converting them as soon as they could. They recognised that sometimes it didn't always work out, and they frequently had to let temps go. It was still quicker than permanent hiring. The team leaders craved to have quality come in, but had clearly made a compromise in order to just get bodies in.

The process in the volume areas was more rigid, and everybody at least *seemed* to know what their role was. That didn't greatly reduce the tension, however, and it felt deeply confrontational between the team leaders who needed the staff and the recruitment team who would provide them. It should be a partnership. It was a desperate situation all round.

Right across the Bank recruitment seemed to just about hang together, but Lucy felt a moderate sense of overwhelm at the challenge in front of her. As she picked her way through the detail she had a growing horror at the candidate experience throughout, a series of messy stages and a process that was held together by the collective impact of failing and nothing else.

Lucy was convinced there was nothing in the process that gave her confidence that they were even close to making the best hires for each role. Then again there was absolutely no way to measure if that feeling was true or not.

THE OPERATING MODEL

One of the problems with discussing an operating model or proposition for resourcing is that many on the outside of recruitment don't see the need. You just advertise, interview and offer, don't you? It's that persistent problem with the perception of resourcing. It just happens, or it's easy, or it's administrative. It all too often isn't considered something that is difficult, strategic, critical or requiring expertise and structure to manage effectively.

Like any important function in any business, it is important for everyone to know what they are doing when it comes to resourcing, whether you call it a set of rules, a process, an operating model or a proposition. A proposition that has expertise at the heart of it, with oversight and accountability.

It is impossible to manage resourcing process, internal, external, temporary or permanent without a clearly defined set of roles and responsibilities that everyone involved uses to deliver what they need to within their capability. A recruitment operating model may be small in scale, but it is complex, representing an entire business. It is marketing, operations, risk management and logistics all in one small team.

What makes it even more complex is that at the heart of this business is people. People at important and sometimes stressful moments in their lives. The candidate is the customer, and the product. In the *manufacturing process* of recruitment, as candidates are processed, the reality is these are people who will respond emotionally to certain things. They will react positively or negatively to situations and unlike other marketing scenarios the balance of power between buyer and seller is less clearly defined. Both sides need to sell and both sides need to buy. Recruitment mechanics are complex.

A further complication is that the *customer* of the process, the hiring manager, may only recruit once or twice a year, be in a rush to get it done, and is not aware of the complexity involved. Alternatively, there are the people in a business who run volume areas and are constantly recruiting. There are managers who want to do it all, and are perfectly capable of staffing their own teams, those who think they know what they are doing but don't, and those who know they don't know. Manager capability, manager ease of use, managerial time and managerial willingness to cooperate with a defined process are key factors.

There is much to be considered in recruitment operating model design. The size of the recruitment team, the tasks of the recruitment team, communication of roles and responsibilities, the candidate view, the manager view. What will the proposition deliver? Just external hiring? Internal career management? Talent processes? Temporary staffing? What are the volumes? What are the levels of seniority to recruit? Locations? To outsource delivery, or build in-house expertise?

As we shall see these questions are intrinsically linked with the need to define what future capability is required.

Stage one was complete for Lucy and she could prepare the report of her findings on the *strategic* elements of resourcing activity. She smiled to herself at the thought that they were strategic, as the simple truth was everything was transactional and tactical. There was no strategy, no idea of what a strategy should be, no real demonstration of any forward-thinking, and an impression that it was all just desperately in the moment. A need was identified, people did stuff and a new person popped into the role.

The employer branding was totally ineffective and was virtually meaningless for Lothian Bank's needs. Planning was poor and unhelpful for resourcing and based in the immediate. The operating model was a shambolic array of loose agreements.

The big problem was that it indicated an overwhelming lack of appreciation for, or understanding of the work that was required to build quality in the bank. Nobody valued what effective resourcing could achieve for them. There was an absence of any thinking about a link between future capability requirements and what people did now. There needed to be a shift in attitude and execution.

Hire Power

CHAPTER 5
CANDIDATE GENERATION

*"Stopping advertising to save money is like stopping your watch
to save time."*

Henry Ford

The headlines were most definitely unnerving. Lucy realised she had an employer branding position that was ineffective. Planning wasn't helpful to the recruitment team. The recruitment operating model was misunderstood, ignored or just scraping by. String and sticky tape all over.

With this picture in mind, Lucy steeled herself for the dive into the detail below. If employer branding was weak, just how did they go about attracting applicants for their vacancies? How then did they make selection decisions? What was the offer and onboarding process like? Sensing none of this would be brilliant, Lucy was particularly fearful of her last area of interrogation. Just what was the candidate experience like?

Lucy turned her attention to the candidate attraction strategy. How was the employer branding work used to inform potential candidates about the available roles? How did Lothian Bank let different markets know about vacancies? How did they use market intelligence to inform media buying? Was there a social media strategy? How did they go about finding good candidates for each individual role?

In fact, the employer branding messages were barely incorporated into anything they did to find candidates for their vacancies. All advertising was for specific vacancies. They did no brand awareness advertising at all, no generic advertising to drive interest to their careers website. This narrow approach was driven in no small part by the way the team worked, and their operating model constraints. They advertised on some online job boards, the occasional piece of press advertising and, of course, used lots of recruitment agencies.

They used a few of the branding buzz phrases in each online advert and the branding imagery when they advertised in the local press for the contact centres, but that was pretty much it. She already knew from the challenges that she was having in the contact centre recruitment that they simply could not attract the numbers and their success ratios were poor. Yet they persisted with the same postings on the same websites.

For head office recruitment Lucy was fully aware that the employer branding message was lost in the noise of all the recruitment agencies and line mangers saying their piece to candidates. The bank certainly had an employer brand in those markets, but not one they had any real influence over, or real knowledge of. Lucy knew what was good about working at Lothian Bank and what the challenges were–but the candidate's view would be through their contact with agency consultants, friends in the bank and line managers. It was a mystery.

They advertised all roles on the company careers page on the website. The website was functional enough, but the link to get to it from the main company website was hidden in the *corporate information* section. She doubted it was found by many people from the home page. The website traffic data indicated as much.

When candidates clicked through to the careers website they were greeted with the smiling faces of the branding work and a tab of options to guide them to *company information*, *training at Lothian Bank*, *our values* and *search for jobs*. She was frustrated to find that any search for jobs was by business area. Basically, the candidate had to know the structure of Lothian Bank and which department was right for them before applying. Not great.

Lucy searched for advertised vacancies and examined a few. She was immediately irritated by the quality. To be fair, the team was always stretched to the limit, but the advertisements for jobs they posted were all just cut and pasted from the role profile. Full of jargon, difficult to understand, rambling, undoubtedly inaccurate and worst of all made no effort to sell—just stated details. She suspected any applicants looked at the role title, salary and location and popped in an application.

This direct sourcing approach was unsurprisingly ineffective. Of course, Lucy couldn't find any data to tell her what the candidate sourcing split was, but she suspected that over 70% of hiring was done externally and of that over 90% was through agencies. Her predecessor had put a preferred supplier list (PSL) in place, but as she realised when looking at the operating model, that was largely an administrative exercise for the purchasing department.

Given they were a major part of the supply chain, Lucy was very interested in how Lothian Bank engaged, and worked with, the agencies. She knew that using an agency may be an expensive way to recruit, but she didn't think it was necessarily bad. Good partnerships with the right agencies in the right markets could make this an effective way of accessing high quality. Particularly in the absence of a coherent employer branding approach to marketing.

After speaking to many of the agency suppliers and the hiring managers she realised that this wasn't the case. There were a range of approaches adopted and many of them had consequences that they didn't realise would impact the calibre of candidates they were seeing.

Some managers played by the rules that were on the intranet and only used the suppliers on the preferred supplier list. However, what Lucy realised in speaking to those suppliers was that often the manager would simply send the role profile (through the ATS) to all five suppliers at once. What Lucy also realised was that by doing a great job in driving rates to a low level for the PSL, the Bank had created an environment whereby they were effectively punished for being compliant. The agencies were always in a *race* with the others on the PSL to submit candidates, and the winner was rewarded with a low fee.

The agency staff didn't deliberately push poor candidates the way of Lothian Bank, but they all had their more junior consultants on the account and given they could earn higher fee income from other accounts on higher rates, Lothian Bank wasn't front and centre of their thinking when they met a superstar.

Low engagement, agencies working with scant detail and delivery by the least experienced consultants. Consultants who would barely understand the business, let alone be able to sell it compellingly. Lucy felt no confidence that they were getting the best service, or the best candidates.

Some managers worked with niche or boutique agencies (as they called themselves) who were specialists in a given field. They purported to know everybody in the industry in whatever their area of expertise was. These managers tended to work with a single consultant and the result was usually a hire that the manager was pleased with. The fees, however, were at a level Lucy found quite eye-watering. It was also a great way for the managers to keep up with the industry gossip and see what was out there for themselves, so they held tight to the relationships.

In between these two extremes Lucy identified a myriad of different approaches and patterns of supplier engagement. There were managers who had favourite suppliers, who offered little in delivery but promised much. Managers who would meet candidates speculatively submitted by any agency under the sun in the hope of finding a star in the random mix. Generally, there was an environment that fostered recruitment agency feeding frenzy.

Where the recruitment team did work hard on sourcing candidates themselves was for the volume areas. A close examination showed Lucy that the careers website adverts for branch and call centre staff were all out of date. The roles had changed, but the role profiles hadn't and the online adverts were simply a copy of the role profile. That in itself was an advertising crime, Lucy thought, but she would come back to that.

There had developed a simple contradiction between what was being advertised and what the jobs had changed to. The advertisements failed to acknowledge any sales element, yet cross-selling of products had been part of the roles for some time. Later, she would find out that sales capability wasn't being assessed for either. No wonder people were leaving so soon, if you don't want to work in sales jobs, you don't apply for sales jobs.

The imagery used in the traditional press advertising only was nice, colourful and appealing, but could really apply to anyone. Smiling faces with headsets on, with a primary colour background. Press advertising did generate a response, particularly from the free paper that people read on the bus. They rarely used it now though, as the pressure on cost forced them to focus on the response they got from online job postings.

For reasons Lucy was all too aware of the predominant approach was becoming temp-to-perm. It was unplanned but somehow it suited everyone. For the recruitment team, the approach helped contribute to the maintenance of the low cost per hire figure, which was their main target. The salary and margin paid for the temporary worker came out of the business operations budget and not the recruitment budget. It pushed the average cost of hiring right down. For the hiring managers, when they were struggling to get permanent staff, it was very easy.

What frustrated Lucy the most was that, on the surface, this led to management reports that showed a slick operation which crushed its cost per hire target. Scratch that away and it was running to stand still and was adopting a warm body approach to quality.

The conclusions for candidate attraction were as obvious as they were bleak. Nothing was based on any real market insight. Old trusted methods that did a job. Inaccurate messaging, and no long-term candidate talent pool building or relationship forming strategy at all. There was no genuine effort to attract high calibre people. It was driven by time and cost. They did not have a strategy at all.

There are really two fundamental candidate challenges facing Lucy in Lothian Bank. Both are commonplace in the real world. Firstly, the approach is all short term. The budget for each item of recruitment is, in essence, attached to that individual vacancy or a campaign. This forces an approach whereby every vacancy or campaign is dealt with in financial isolation, creating a problem for any budgeting for long-term resourcing strategy. The funding for long-term projects often needs to be derived from a cost saving in the execution. Cost savings in execution can lead to cutting corners and an assault on quality.

The second problem is tactically where and how Lothian communicates with its potential employees to sell the vacancies. The primary methods are through agencies and with the use of online postings. Where recruitment is handled in a vacancy-to-vacancy transactional manner these are the typical approaches. Even tactically these approaches can be executed effectively in the search for great staff, or not.

What are the merits and pitfalls of the Lothian Bank tactical approach? After all, this approach is precisely the recruitment deployment approach for so many different organisations.

THE ONLINE JOB POSTING

For a start, the typical online advertisement is usually where recruitment meets the role profile. A role profile, or job description, and perhaps a person specification, is the description of each role in an organisation, what the duties are and what is required by the role holder to perform those duties. This then forms the basis of much of the information used to advertise, select and assess. What it is not is an appealing and interesting description of why someone might want to do the role.

Inaccuracies in the role profile are frequent. Do you have role profiles for every role in your business? Are they up to date? Are they accurate? Is anyone responsible for making sure they are? Accuracy of the role profile is a problem for most organisations. As a basis for advertising it is an obvious starting point, but it has limitations. In the product marketing world, that would be like the marketing manager taking an out-of-date product description as the basis for the campaign.

You don't have to look hard on recruitment websites to find examples of what this looks like and just how uninspiring this approach is. Below are random examples from a leading careers website.

The first two are for a marketing manager and (ironically) a recruitment manager. You can guess what the third one is.

These haven't been pulled because they are particularly awful examples, or outliers in the way roles are advertised. Any search on the internet will quickly yield many such examples. They demonstrate why the role profile as an advert has limitations. The typos are from the originals, and not editorial oversight.

ADVERTISEMENT I—MARKETING

- Develop integrated marketing communication plans that support COMPANY objectives

- Manage the implementation of multi-channel marketing campaigns that build COMPANY brand awareness and drives new leads

- Coordinate marketing communications across all aspects of the COMPANY business in order to attract potential customers, retain existing ones and meet strategic objectives

- Maintain regular, ongoing communications with internal and external stakeholders in order to keep them updated on marketing communications campaigns, including outcomes

- Adjust campaign plans and initiatives as required

- Measure the return on investment of marketing communications across different aspects of the business and the impact of brand awareness campaigns with our members, prospective members, and other key stakeholders

- Ensure all marketing activities conform to brand guidelines and positioning and champion brand discipline within the COMPANY

- Take responsibility for effective use of the marketing budget ensuring marketing communications campaigns are completed on budget and according to budget guidelines

- Provide regular status reports on all aspects of the role including budget and return on investment

- Work closely with others in the Communications Team to ensure alignment and consistency of messaging

- Leverage industry and marketing communications research/best practice in order to improve the effectiveness of marketing communications campaigns and initiatives

- Line management responsibility as directed

- Any other duties that may be reasonably required

ADVERTISEMENT 2–RECRUITMENT MANAGER

- Responsible for the complete end-to-end recruitment and selection process including; sourcing, screening, pre-qualification, interviewing and final candidate selection.

- Translate business objectives into robust recruiting strategies and routes to market.

- Design and deliver innovative sourcing strategies and solutions to meet business needs; generate talent pipeline using a variety of channels, social media, data mining, and x-ray searching.

- Develop multi-hire sourcing strategies and collaborate with colleagues cross-divisionally and cross-functionally to leverage wide channels, and coordinate global campaigns.

- Work in partnership with the hiring managers and HR community to understand and drive resource planning, and to define appropriate timescales for recruitment campaigns.

- Provide consultative services on industry and market trends to the business.

- Conduct competency-based interviews with candidates at final interview and provide hiring recommendations to the business.

- Analyse dashboards, reports and BI to proactively monitor and interpret internal and external conditions, using these findings to deliver operational excellence and continuous improvement

ADVERTISEMENT 3–

- Business facing Service Managers aligned to each COMPANY business unit and via them the end users themselves

- Delivery and Service managers within the technical teams involved in delivering service, to drive a culture of trend analysis and ongoing improvement via Problem Management

- 3rd party service providers to ensure effective and constructive collaboration exist to manage trend and address incidents and restore service as an absolute priority

- Business IT at COMPANY locations across the globe to drive best practice and potentially shared resourcing for global service delivery

- Close liaison with Service Desk ensuring two-way communication is effective, timely and accurate. This will include decisions on appropriate broadcasts, utilisation of VIP routing within desk, etc.

- Provision of focused MI regarding the number, severity and resultant actions fro (sic) incident

The final example could describe any number of jobs. Without the role title, it is quite difficult to understand what it is. Some of the descriptions don't make any sense out of context at all.

At first glance, it is easy to forgive the failings of these advertisements. They describe the roles and without the company jargon they give a flavour for what the tasks are. They make sense until you think about what these advertisements are attempting to achieve.

Of course, if you know what the list of activities in these adverts mean, then you know what the job is. There is much in the descriptions that cover things that are common to all these roles in every organisation. If you are selling a car, you don't start with a description of four wheels, engine, gearbox, suspension, front window, indicators etc. That's not selling the car, it's telling you what a car is. If you are looking to buy a car, you already probably know what a car is and what it does. If you don't know, then arguably you shouldn't be buying a car. The information serves little purpose.

Yes, the detail is important for a candidate as they go through the process, but at the front end there is a level of detail that is required and a level of making the role sound appealing that is essential. When I buy a car, the boot space is important, but the precise dimensions of the boot are unlikely to be in the advert I see on television. Perhaps, a large dog in the boot, perhaps a set of football kits, a happy family with fun beach equipment— something that shows how a big boot will make my life better. Not its dimensions. Bullet point job descriptions are mostly all dimensions.

Do candidates read these details? Are they a mental checklist of, "Yes, I can do that, done that, I'll wing that... Done that..."? What do they feel about the opportunity when they see these adverts? Does such a long list of statements actually put some highly capable people off? Internal advertisements are usually worse. At least external job postings usually have an opening paragraph of positive (possibly linked to the employer brand) statements about the employer. Internal advertising is usually just the role profile posted on an internal job board. The jargon may be understood, and the language may be familiar, but does it excite and communicate what the role is about? For people wishing to make a move internally, role understanding is only achieved through informal communication—in other words, having a coffee with someone in the department.

Sometimes when you look at the volume and quality of online job postings, you have to ask yourself has anyone actually ever read what they have written/copied and pasted? Is this indicative of a lack of awareness, time, or thought? Is it arrogance and confidence in the consumer brand to do the selling work? Or is it just the way things are done, and if everyone does the same then no harm will come.

Why is a practice that has confused and misled candidates for the last twenty-five years on the internet still dominant? And this is the dominant approach. Job board posting is the primary route to market for most roles in most businesses.

The Lothian Bank example of the advertisement for the contact centre role missing a critical piece of information about the role isn't unrealistic.

Retail Business C ran a recruitment process whereby they had a centralised recruitment team that selected staff to start and the branch manager was delivered his new starter as and when required. Great, except the role evolved and the recruitment team hadn't caught up, as demonstrated in the words of one new joiner, "I didn't know that sales was a part of the job, but I don't mind. It's ok. I'm learning."

That was someone who saw an advert, went through an application and interview and only when she was in the role did she become aware of a key skill that was required. They quite literally only found out about a key skill for the job on day one.

The sales element wasn't huge, but it was enough to make the job appeal to a different mindset and take a different approach to be successful. Management in the business thought that the sales element was obvious. The HR team worked from the information they had. In the constant tactical delivery cycle there was a breakdown in communication.

Staff joined and then some staff left to do the customer service jobs elsewhere that they thought they were going to do. All the recruitment effort, not to mention the experience for the new staff, was jeopardised through an oversight in detail.

RECRUITMENT AGENCIES

As in all supply and demand environments there is a broker in recruitment that will bridge the gap between supply and demand. The recruitment agency industry.

A big challenge for Lothian Bank with head office and IT candidate generation was the reliance on agency recruitment. In many recruitment functions, there is a natural desire to reduce agency usage as much as possible. After all, at a cost per hire of about 15-20% of the starting salary, it's certainly potentially expensive. An expense that can be justified against the absence of someone delivering, and that the buyer has become accustomed to.

Despite the growth of direct sourcing teams in large organisations and this pressure on costs the demise of the recruitment agency has been frequently exaggerated. Their world may have changed, and many principals in agencies will talk about pressure on fees, candidates being harder to find, competition from social media, but the reality is that a quick scroll on the internet reveals there are still thousands of thriving recruitment businesses. The barriers to entry are low, and the market still demands the presence of the broker.

Why is this, when essentially, they do little radically different from the in-house recruiter? Surely social media, particularly LinkedIn, has completely shifted the balance away from the agencies? There are multiple reasons this hasn't happened, and mostly they are based in the way people think and behave through a recruitment process. As long as it is people who recruit other people there is space for brokerage. The secret for organisations is to understand what suppliers they will need, work with them, not against and derive greater value from the relationship. Make a conscious decision about the use of agencies, not treat it as the default.

The human factors come from all sides. Take the candidate view. Some scan the job boards, see a job title they want with a company they know and send off their CV. Some do huge amounts of research, understand what they want, target the companies and make direct speculative approaches. Some people sit back and move after they are approached by a headhunter, or by their former boss. There is the senior level kudos in being headhunted. Some go to the job centre. People use their networks. Some people scan the paper on the bus into work, and see what's paying more. There are lots of ways that *hook* a candidate.

Then there is the sort of candidate that frankly can't be bothered with all that trouble to look and apply. The lazy jobseeker. He will have a relationship with a consultant who works for a recruitment firm and when they fancy a move they call him up and he then makes calls on their behalf. Bob's your uncle, a couple of interviews and an offer. Don't make the mistake of assuming that a lazy jobseeker is a lazy employee. This can easily be a candidate who works in a niche area and he knows the recruitment consultant who mines that seam, and that makes it very easy for both. They may be flat out busy, and want the help to find a new job. They may not know the market. It can easily be that it is the known way to get to certain employers.

The hiring manager needs results quickly as she has just had a resignation. There is an HR process to be dealt with, but then there is that specialist agency that she knows well (after all, they placed her in her last job) and they have *good people on their books*. (A phrase much beloved of any in-house recruitment consultant.) Plus, she has a belief that the agency will be much quicker than HR, and she can always do the paperwork afterwards.

Regardless of the strength of HR governance and policy, there is very little stopping someone from calling a recruitment consultant and asking them for a couple of CVs when they have a gap. The view is often that, yes, this may get a slapped wrist from HR, but that is a price worth paying. The belief that an agency is quicker and they have good people may be a falsehood, but a belief is a belief nonetheless.

The manager may well also be thinking about their career. It's good to keep the network alive, and stay in touch with the consultants in the sector, after all, you never know when they might come in handy.

The final protagonist is the recruitment consultant. Potentially high earning, but often on a low basic wage. It's a sales-based commission business and they earn commission on getting people hired. Hired, regardless of how suitable or good they are. However, to say they don't care about how suitable or good the placement is, is a misrepresentation. They have professional pride, and placing good people enhances the chances of repeat business. Repeat business is easier to win than new business. Yes, they care about quality, but the driver is different. They need to sell, and sell they will. They put a very positive slant on what they do, the candidate relationships they have, how they assess people and their reach and speed. It's a good sales pitch for a distress purchase. Never be in doubt that these businesses are in the sales business.

The commodity they are selling here is a person and they can enhance their chances of success by working with that person. They will coach the candidate through the recruitment process. A good consultant recognises a good candidate, not for the positive contribution they will make for your business, but for the fact that they are a *walking score*. They certainly can add value and they are certainly part of the supply chain, and an important channel if understood and integrated properly.

Agencies then will play a part in the recruitment for most businesses to a greater or lesser extent. That extent is determined by planning and trust in the planning as much as it is down to the human factors. They are not the only answer nor are they not an answer, they sit with every other channel used to access candidates. Knowing the right channel to access the right candidates is the secret to candidate generation at a tactical level.

TEMP-TO-PERM

Recruiting people as temporary staff and then converting them to permanent roles holds an attraction for many organisations, particularly in the fast-moving volume recruitment markets. Lothian Bank fell into it almost by default, but is this a wise strategy?

It indicates a couple of things. Firstly, a lack of confidence in permanent recruitment processes. Secondly, it indicates less than perfect planning. There is immediacy in the appointment of temporary staff. Immediacy that indicates the plan isn't working.

The *try-before-you-buy* is the appeal. It suits an organisational driver. If they don't work out, we can get rid of them and summon a replacement. However, it is worth considering the consequences of the approach before embracing it.

It sends a message about the type of employer you are. One who commoditises the lowest paid members of the team. (As they will be.) It is a narrow market. A narrow market that restricts you from hiring those people who want permanency in the role. And it actually isn't a very nice way to think about people. We know the candidate experience and the recruitment of high-quality staff are linked. This is not a great way to think about people, and not a great experience for joining a company.

As a strategy, it has limitations. As a tactical opportunity for someone who joins a business as a temporary member of staff, performs well and is offered a permanent role, well, that makes sense. Most businesses will have need for temporary staff and some of them will want to join the business in a permanent capacity. Where the permanent role exists that makes perfect sense. The consideration then is how to manage the transition. Appoint? Interview? Insist they apply like everyone else? No right answer— but the wrong answer is to not have an approach.

The approach adopted by Lothian Bank is common. There is tactical deployment of recruitment tools to react to a vacancy, or campaign. The quickly assembled internet posting, the distribution of a role to multiple badly briefed recruitment agencies and a scattergun approach on LinkedIn. This passes for a strategy for generating candidates.

When the strategy isn't in place the time pressure on tactics will produce behaviour and activity that will not improve the chances of attracting quality applications. There is no universal right way, or wrong way. However, a planned approach will get better results than a forced approach. A planned approach based on understanding of your organisation's needs, gaps and the markets in which it exists.

Driven by a plan, every channel for product advertising can be used, and has been used for recruitment advertising, be that brand building or role advertising. There are the job postings, recruitment agencies, traditional press advertising, trade press advertising, bus shelters, billboards, bus tickets, flyers, radio, television, public relations. Even the backs of petrol pump handles, or on heavy goods vehicle sides. All ways of touching the candidate with a message.

Candidate generation of the right people is critical and needs thought, rather than reaction. If you don't get quality at the outset then what happens next is irrelevant. There is an old computer programming saying of *garbage in, garbage out*. Although it is unkind to apply that idiom to a people process, the sentiment is essentially true.

A compelling message makes the people who are the best fit and match want to work for you, so speak to them in a way that makes it easy to understand that message. When it comes to generating applications of the right people to the business, the key must be understanding the behaviours of the candidate populations you are interested in. Market data. The data aligned to the knowledge of the recruiter provides insight into the markets and the guidance as to which channels to exploit. There isn't a single answer, there are multiple answers and the only way to identify the balance of cost against time against quality is to understand the market. Understand the movements and behaviours of people in the market. Treat them like individuals. That's how product marketers think.

Hire Power

CHAPTER 6
SELECTION

"Time! The corrector when our judgments err."

Lord Byron

Lucy spent a lot of time sitting in on interviews and watching assessment centres to understand how selection decisions were made at Lothian Bank. She no longer had high expectations of encountering anything that was leading edge, though what she observed was disappointing, even by modest expectations. At times, she struggled to contain her disbelief. Her initial concerns about tools, governance and capability were illustrated in interviewing and assessment in stark relief.

For volume recruitment, the overall approach to assessment was one that she liked. The applicants were initially screened against a set of criteria, and those that failed to meet the standards were rejected. The remainder were booked into an assessment centre, where they undertook a series of exercises, scored by team leaders from the contact centres. Multiple data sets and multiple pairs of eyes to validate. This was good. A scored assessment centre, based on set criteria and all candidates going through the same experience is the fairest and most objective method of evaluation.

Lucy found the issues quickly once she delved deeper than the principles of approach. She was troubled by the screening. Candidates for the roles submitted a CV and filled in their online application form. The online form asked some *killer* questions with certain answers that would knock the candidate straight out (criminal record, availability for the shift patterns, etc.). The form also asked the candidate to describe their working experience and skills. As her team screened out the applicants they didn't wish to proceed to assessment, they did so on the content of this application form. What did they do with the CV, she wondered.

Lucy also wondered why the selection criteria they used had been chosen. The screening process was designed to reduce the high number of applicants but Lucy was puzzled by some of the screening criteria. In particular, they only took people with previous financial services' experience, eliminating lots of potentially good customer service people. She discovered that the reason was that the time from joining to going on the phones was supposedly too short for the training team to upskill with knowledge of the industry. A compromise that seemed based on poor planning.

They advanced the candidates who met the criteria for financial services' experience, the high education bar and availability to the assessment centre. They always overbooked the assessment centre, as they always experienced a lot of candidates who didn't show up. Lucy was surprised that the event was a full-day session, which seemed like a significant time investment by the candidate.

When they were short on candidates through direct applications for slots at the assessment centre, they used a local agency partner to supply candidates to fill the vacant slots, trusting them to screen to the same level.

The assessment centre itself was the standard bank format they had used for years. The tests were the same as they'd always been and were based on the defined competencies for customer service staff throughout the bank. When was the last time they validated how these competencies related to the actual job? Had they evaluated the characteristics of top performers in designing them? Turned out *no*, and *no*. They were long-standing and based on what management in the distant past thought were likely to be the best indicators.

Mark, the volume recruitment manager, knew the numbers and ratios required for success in contact centre recruitment and Lucy had always been impressed with his grasp of the detail. For every hire, they knew they needed fifteen applications. They screened out ten of the applicants, so that for every five people they invited to assessment centre, they hired one. This ratio rang loud alarm bells in Lucy's head. Mark was so flat out getting the numbers in, he hadn't had the time to stop and check if they were doing the right thing.

They always struggled with numbers though, and the shortfall was made up with temps. They didn't go through any assessment, so it was easier to join as a temp and take the chance of being converted to permanent. The whole assessment approach seemed rather redundant. The wheels were turned furiously to recruit, but quality of hire was under attack from all sides.

The problem to take back to Chris for volume recruitment was easily explained. The ratio of pass to fail at the centre was too high, wasting time and irritating the team leaders. The exercises were no longer fit for purpose and needed to be changed to reflect the demands of the role. The team leaders had never been trained in assessment and each approached the task slightly differently.

There was no focus on the candidate experience, and the full day was much too much to ask of entry-level staff. It was also unnecessary, given the simplicity of the role. She saw the need for a full role evaluation, which could make screening and selection much more effective.

What was encouraging was that there were some obvious and easy quick wins for improvements.

VOLUME RECRUITMENT ASSESSMENT

The assessment of high volumes of people to do the same, often a customer facing role, is one of the critical front-line tasks of any resourcing function. That means recruiting the right people to do these jobs, and giving them the right training. These jobs are low-level, low-paid and repetitive, from warehouse picking to production lines, baristas or retail staff, but of undoubted importance to the business and to the customer experience. The calibre of people at the front end makes all the difference—good or bad.

The example of Lothian Bank may be fictional, but it isn't an exaggeration. In fact, they adopted what is widely recognised as the best approach to large-scale or volume assessment—the assessment centre—so the principle of approach is good. A variety of exercises, linked to role performance, measuring different capabilities or competencies and viewed by multiple assessors. It helps if the criteria are actually linked to the role, however.

The mistakes Lucy encountered are examples of common issues in the volume recruitment environment. It isn't always an easy environment to define assessment for. The *hard*, easily definable technical requirements are limited in the success criteria for these types of roles. Success, or otherwise, will come down to the individual's attitude, or behaviours, or a few key attributes.

Therein lies a trap. A tendency to pick criteria for assessment that don't relate directly to a measurement of success for the role.

Often what is perceived to be a critical competency for the role, just isn't.

Company A is a Middle East services business. On launching an industry leading online customer service and sales product they decided that their customer service staff must have a significant social media presence. The product was marketed online and through social media, so the thinking went that the staff would need to understand how the channels worked.

What the members of staff did was open accounts for customers and solve basic queries. They never needed or accessed social media at work. In fact, analysis revealed that there was no correlation whatsoever between the social media activity and customer service skills, even in their social media service offering.

What the staff needed was an ability to understand the customer problem and solve it, regardless of the channel for communicating the problem. However, candidates were eliminated from the process if they didn't meet a certain level of social media activity—Instagram followers, twitter presence, etc., without exception.

Sometimes there is a desire to be quirky. To be different for the sake of being different. To believe that a curiosity in assessment will reveal that special characteristic you desire. There is most certainly a place for creativity, and different thinking in assessment, but it can go too far...

Company B, an online retailer, wanted staff to be sociable and have a sense of humour. The job was repetitive, and they wanted high spirits in the face of adversity.

They invited their recruitment supplier to design something that reflected their innovation and the completely different and *wacky* working environment they were creating.

The supplier met the brief and included an assessment exercise to measure the candidate's sense of humour. They asked each candidate to watch ten minutes of *Kung Fu Panda II*. They assessed reaction by watching the candidates watch the clip. Laughter at certain parts got the candidate good marks.

No explanation of why this demonstrates a poor correlation to job performance is necessary. Obviously, that's because the original *Kung Fu Panda* is much better.

In another retail business, **Company C**, they wanted to hire people who had a strong customer service bent. Perfectly sensible.

In the opening interview of the assessment centre, the interviewer would drop his pen. Those who picked it up, were progressed in the assessment centre. Those who didn't, weren't. This was taken as an indicator of each individual's customer service attitude.

The reality is that an exercise contrived to see who will pick up the interviewer's pen in an interview scenario, will identify only one thing for sure. One thing that may not ever come in useful in the workplace. It will identify who is going to pick up the interviewer's pen, on that day, in that interview.

These are all quite extreme examples. The criteria didn't reflect the reality of the role and the exercises didn't correlate with the criteria. To assess for a role there needs to be a link to what success looks like in that role. An assessment of the characteristics and behaviours that indicate the individual will repeat them in role.

Company D, an insurance company ran a similar format of assessment centre to that of Lothian Bank for their contact centre staff and had teamwork included as one of the core competencies for their volume recruitment.

The job itself entailed being on a telephone talking to customers for seven hours a day. It wasn't a difficult environment, with the calls mostly being renewals and queries about a policy. However, they struggled to recruit sufficient numbers of staff to manage the turnover.

A major reason was that people were failing the high bar in assessment for the *teamwork and collaboration* competency. The reason for the high bar? The centre manager firmly believed in, and promoted a team-based culture. During major sporting events, like the World Cup, they all flew flags of the competing nations above their desks and had league tables of which team was most effective. They held problem-solving sessions involving different people from various teams, and encouraged a team-based social life. They fostered a healthy rivalry and a lively environment.

This was all laudable. It was a nice place to work. However, the measure of teamworking in the assessment process had no real bearing whatsoever on effectiveness in role. Analysis of those who were most participative in the team culture against the assessment revealed no correlation. Likewise, there was no correlation with the teamworking criteria and high performance. High performers were more likely to have performed well in the problem-solving and resilience competencies.

Downgrading the emphasis on teamworking measures, without eliminating them, kept the centre manager happy, and in a single moment reduced the pressure of recruitment numbers. No complaints about quality or effect on the environment followed. The teamworking culture was created by the manager and people naturally fell into it.

Another common issue is overthinking the process. The jobs aren't complex and the success criteria aren't complex. There is a balance to be sought between identifying the characteristics, not making the candidate's experience too onerous, and getting to the heart of what is required.

Plus, when you deal with large volumes of applicants, there needs to be an *industrialisation* of the process, with an understanding of the individual. That means you have to be able to measure it, within an experience that doesn't make the human being at the centre feel like a commodity.

For **company E**, a large and well-known UK-wide retailer the problem was that the leaders of the business had agreed on a set of criteria that were difficult to measure for their front-of-house staff recruitment.

Apart from the fact that the terminology for the characteristic was slightly (actually, very) regrettable, the characteristics they settled on were subjective. Their acronym for their ideal target employee was BEAVER: bright, enthusiastic, attractive, versatile, energetic and reliable.

See the problem? They aren't bad criteria (except *attractive*, of course—that's just not something that needs any further explanation) for what success looks like in a retail environment. However, just a little thought reveals that they are mostly open to individual interpretation.

The truth of the matter is that they were all clumped together in a managerial gut feel of the *right sort*. It is indicative of the clash between what the academic view of assessment is and what some front-line managers *feel* they want.

Company F, a media company, is an example of an organisation that would overcomplicate the activity.

They were at the opposite end of the spectrum, they forensically analysed the results of the assessment centre to the extreme. They gave each competency in each exercise a score, and then created a set of averages at the end. They took this average to two decimal points. Additionally, they manipulated the data by removing certain exercises from individuals' scores, if they performed well in that competency in another test. Then recalculated.

Certainly, they weren't talking the decision lightly, but can we really measure the complexity of human behaviour in the artificial surroundings of an assessment centre to two decimal places?

Probably not.

With her mixed view of the volume process documented, Lucy turned attention to head office and IT. The problem with head office assessment was much the same as it was with candidate generation. One of a multitude of local approaches, and loose governance. The recruitment team, usually working with an agency, endeavoured to provide enough CVs for the manager to take three candidates forward to interview. The interview itself would be left to the manager to conduct.

As well as a manager's technical discussion with the candidate, Lothian Bank used competency-based interviewing as standard for head office and technical recruitment. They had a list of competencies (standard corporate stuff, as Lucy observed) that formed the performance matrix for all staff. For interview the manager decided what competencies they wanted to assess on and HR would send them the structured interview pack to complete during the interview.

The final task for the manager at the end of the interview would be to update the job on the ATS recording who was successful and who wasn't. The system would automatically send out declines and the recruitment team would re-enter the process to make the offer.

Like all moving parts processes there were bits that Lucy didn't particularly like. She was troubled by document storage and governance after interview. She knew full well that the manager ATS updates would be fairly hit-and-miss. She didn't much like the idea of interview packs floating around, when they were also used for internal interviews.

However, the real problem she had was with the managers being left to conduct the interview with the guidance of the interview material and little else. Some, usually the inexperienced ones, would seek help from the recruiters, but most hiring managers progressed with the interview confident in their ability to make the right choice. There was nothing in place to monitor the capability of those interviewing, or what they covered in the interviews. It felt like a risk.

Not that the hiring managers were all bad interviewers, but the quality of interviewing would be wildly inconsistent across the population. Lucy sat in on a number of interviews and she really did see a range of approaches and a range of dubious decisions. There were good, bad and indifferent levels of interviewing capability; managers who didn't understand and counteract their own bias, managers who thought that they were deep experts but reacted to gut instinct, managers who merrily followed their bias. (*This candidate is like me, and I've done well.*)

In the mix, there were also those who understood that what they wanted to do was gain a holistic view of which candidates would perform in the role successfully, and make a decision based on that and that alone.

Not one manager wanted to make a poor decision, but too many of them stumbled to a decision because they simply didn't know better, trusted their experience, or followed what they had read on a blog entitled *ten ways to spot the perfect candidate*. Lucy observed many had their own favourite trick question that they liked to catch candidates with.

Yes, some made excellent decisions and some made poor ones. For many it was impossible to tell if a better decision was possible, and that was the point. Uncertainty was built into the process. The attraction process was uninspiring. The rigour in assessment was totally variable. These factors fundamentally meant that Lothian Bank had surrendered the probability of hiring well, and therefore improving overall capability to virtual chance.

"Even a blind squirrel finds an acorn, once in a while," thought Lucy as she reviewed her findings.

It was entirely what she expected, but it was also entirely dispiriting, nonetheless. There was no way of knowing what damage was being done. How many hires were made that wouldn't fit, how many great people were declined for not getting the trick questions *right*? Yet again, Lucy realised the business just didn't know about the problem it was facing.

For both head office and for the volume recruitment Lucy reflected yet again, that they needed better tools, better capability and better governance to make these things stick. Above all, she had a *hearts-and-minds* selling job to do to convince the business that resourcing was something worth putting more thought, effort and time into.

The problem Lucy was faced with in head office was a population of variable skills undertaking a selection process with little formal training. They didn't care much for the governance and were using tools they didn't fully respect or use properly.

THE INTERVIEW

In simple, monetary terms, what a hiring manager is doing is making a purchase, and a significant corporate purchase at that. Hiring someone into an organisation at £50,000 per year is an ongoing annual cost and you can pretty much add an extra 50% on for space, technology, benefits, etc. If that manager was buying an IT system at an annual fee of £75,000 on a permanent contract the due diligence and governance surrounding that buying decision would be significant. In fact, it would probably involve a technical needs analysis, a defined tendering process against a rigid specification and sign-off at a higher authority.

Not three chats of one hour, some of which was about hobbies and the weather and a follow-up chat with the boss. Yet, somehow in the *purchase* of the people resource the decision is considered less worthy of control. Why? That goes back to the respect for the business of resourcing, and how easy so many *think* that it is.

Company G is a retail organisation—not the *BEAVER* one, but similar in scale. They also had an interesting quirk in their recruitment.

Interviews were the only form of assessment used, and they prioritised two parts of the interview over all others. Firstly, they had *Golden Questions*. These were little random interview hand grenades, deliberately designed to throw the candidate off balance. For example—"If you were an animal, what kind of animal would you be and why?"

The second trick was to continue casually asking questions on the way back to the exit after the interview, particularly about what they didn't like in their current role. The candidate was off guard then. When the candidate thought the interview was over, the hiring manager thought they were getting the most insight, placing the most emphasis on this section.

These things weren't linked to job performance, so actually had no predictive validity, but the managers liked it. It was a sort of pseudo-science. What was really happening was that they were trusting gut instinct, or going by the CV, or gravitating towards their unconscious bias (that we all have).

It was justified on the grounds of seeing the candidate *at their most honest*. That ignores any idea that an interview can be a difficult and stressful experience, or that the candidate might say what they think you want to hear on the way to the lift, or a list of other possibilities. It was certainly a strange approach, and above all else, completely unfair to the candidate.

So, did this business go bust because they hired consistently rubbish people? In fact, did the pen dropping company end up folding? Or the guys who only recruited *beavers*? Surely if we are to believe the life's work of recruitment experts and occupational psychologists, then this slapdash approach yields nothing but disaster?

The assumption that a bad process only ever recruits bad people and a good process only ever recruits good people is missing the point. This is about *maximising* the probability of getting good people and recruiting the best capability. Even grabbing random people off the street to do any job will eventually yield a result... Lucy's idiom about blind squirrels and acorns.

The point is that to take the long-term capability building view of the organisation as a whole, it's the marginal increases in probability at every stage that makes the difference. The assessment stage happens to be one of those that has scientific measures around it and has a measurable impact. Settling for chance is settling to put the bar at random, average, ok.

BIAS

There are two types of bias in recruitment, conscious and unconscious. Conscious bias is easy to spot. "I don't recruit gingers, because they are useless." This is a perfect example of conscious bias, and a particularly odious one too.

Unconscious bias is the more prevalent and damaging form. Prevalent because it exists in everybody. That's right, everybody. There is something about some subset of humanity that will provoke a generalising train of thought in everyone. You see a group of bikers. A heavily tattooed woman. A ginger-headed guy. Fat people. Someone in a wheelchair. The trick is not to be seduced into thinking that this bias you possess is an indicator of how someone else will perform in the job. Damaging, because it is very common and much more subtle, therefore tougher to identify and tackle.

Don't blame yourself, or hiring managers, for possessing unconscious bias. There are real scientifically understood psychological reasons for the existence of bias. It is what a psychologist might call a cognitive shortcut. It probably helped when the tribe in the next valley was constantly trying to steal your cave. Of course, that doesn't make it a helpful thing in the modern business environment.

As such, understanding, and then dealing with, unconscious bias is an important factor in successful assessment. Aside from the obvious moral (and legal) positions, it's simply not in an organisation's best interest to have segments of society excluded through bias. When you want the best people, denying yourself whole tranches of society that don't fit the description for utterly irrational, and not performance-based, reasons is simply an assault on your chances of getting it right.

The only bias that you should follow is a bias towards who is most likely to be best in the role. You only get that through gathering evidence about probable performance.

Lucy's journey through the effectiveness of the department continued with the offer and onboarding process, and yet again she wasn't surprised to find that, whilst things worked, they had come about by accident rather than design. The reward manager at Lothian Bank had set pay bands for all the levels, and would benchmark each role as required. The benchmark would be based on market data, and he used a well-known, reliable reward consultancy for the benchmarking.

What Lucy observed was that whilst the bank's average salaries were pretty much on benchmark, head office new hires tended to fare much better. Initially she thought that was just a bump for moving, but as she looked closer at the data the high level of hiring through agencies was definitely a factor. All within acceptable bands, but all at the upper levels of the bands. It certainly meant that very few head office hires rejected the bank at offer stage.

THE OFFER

Lucy was facing a truism when it comes to making a job offer that can cause upward pressure on salaries. It's very simple and again, human nature is at the heart of it. In the offer equation, there are two or three, possibly four or maybe five people involved. There is the hiring manager and the candidate, of course. Then there is the agency consultant and the in-house recruiter. There may also be someone from the reward team involved, to give *a view*.

The candidate will speak to the agency consultant, who will in turn speak to the manager. A discussion about money can be awkward for some people with a prospective new employer, but it certainly isn't awkward for them to discuss with a recruitment consultant, or for the consultant to discuss with the employer. Bear in mind, the consultant gets more commission the higher the salary. However, the consultant gets no commission for a failed negotiation, so they have a balance to find. A balance that guarantees a *yes* from the candidate.

So, the candidate aims high in dealings with the consultant and suggests an aspirational figure. The consultant tempers that, but goes to the hiring manager with the words, "You'll definitely get him for x." x is high, but not too high. The manager who is in a bind, given he has had a vacancy for three months and is under pressure, just cannot afford to lose the candidate. The in-house recruiter has a desk of jobs to fill and wants the position successfully closed, and the reward manager is a consultative voice only. No one is gaming the system and no one is trying it on, but human nature ensures the pressure on salary is always upwards pressure, even when there is strong governance around salary setting. In itself that has a financial impact on any business.

By the time Lucy reviewed the onboarding of people into new positions from both internal moves or from external hiring, she was prepared for what she saw. Some managers did it well, and made sure their new joiner was operational and made to feel welcome from day one. In the contact centres the operations teams provided a week-long induction for all new starters before training, and team leaders had huge experience in integrating new staff.

For many in head office their first few days were frustrating; a lack of access to IT systems, discomfort in not knowing who people were and days, sometimes weeks, of feeling directionless. There were stories in the branch network of people turning up on a day when the branch manager was off, and nobody knowing who they were. For young people in junior roles this was often distressing. It was more often absent or poor than good throughout. Simply not in anyone's thinking. Recruitment done, move on.

As Lucy mulled over her concerns for recruitment at Lothian Bank, she knew she would have to present some uncomfortable realities. The processes were vague and ungoverned. Technology usage wasn't optimised. Line mangers didn't have a clear and unified view of what they were doing, let alone any belief that the HR processes could help them. Capability of line managers in observing the process, interviewing, making an offer and onboarding was low. Not because they were incapable, but because it wasn't a priority. For most, recruitment wasn't something they saw as part of their role. They certainly didn't see value add in the recruitment team, and Lucy could hardly blame them. The whole effort of recruitment was about filling the gaps and there was little she could see that was designed to achieve the maximum in quality hiring.

The very last thing that she did was to speak to new joiners throughout the business. She tried to piece together what it was like for them when they were candidates, trying to secure a job with Lothian Bank. Lucy was fully aware of the impact of a good candidate experience, and how that kept the good people in the process, when they easily had choices elsewhere.

It was the first encounter many people had with an organisation, beyond the brand or customer experience. If the candidate experience was attentive, efficient and easy, it created a great impression on joining. It also improved the chances of keeping good people engaged, giving those who started a positive opening experience. A bad candidate experience has a more profound impact. As well as potentially driving the candidate away, they are rather more likely to tell all their friends about how awful the business is, and that they never wanted to work there in the first place.

Lothian Bank candidates did not get anything like a great experience. It was a litany of delays as CVs were being reviewed, no feedback after interview, long gaps in the process, candidates chasing for answers, delayed start dates as the screening was slow, laptops not ready... the list went on. But Lucy knew this in advance. She knew what the impact of all the problems she had already seen would be on the candidate experience. She knew what impact a poor candidate experience was having on their ability to make the best hiring decisions. Yet again, quality pushed down the priority list by not understanding the consequences of actions.

At the same time as Lucy was slogging her way through the recruitment processes analysis, Chris and Simon worked together picking through executive recruitment and talent management. Although talent spotting and the completion of a talent grid (performance on the x-axis against potential on the y-axis) was conducted for all managers in the business, it really only meant anything at senior level.

The managers at mid-level who fastidiously completed talent mapping for their direct reports to discuss with their HR business partner really were just conducting a paper exercise. They were completely wasting their time, although they didn't know it. There had been a plan to do something with all the data, but rolling out the identification process to the managers was where it stopped. It was never implemented further, or any real explanations given to the managers as to what was done, or not done with the information. This gap in delivery was a cloud that hung over Simon's reputation with Chris. They both knew it.

At senior level, the talent mapping took on a more serious purpose. The senior manager population was where the next level of directors would come from. The director population was where the next executives would come from. That was the plan. It was frustrating for Chris that they did so much senior level recruitment. Except for operations, pretty much every time they had a director resign the conversation always turned towards an external search. The executive didn't seem to trust that their senior managers could make the leap.

Yes, there were some people in senior management roles who were certainly very talented individuals and would have great careers, but all too often they moved on to the bigger banks, or weren't considered for the next big roles because they didn't have the relevant experience. Not enough leadership experience, not enough senior sponsorship, or hasn't had enough exposure to the regulator. There always seemed to be something that blotted someone's copybook. The external candidate always had immaculate history.

Chris often wondered if the gap between senior manager and director was really as broad in some areas as the director would have her believe. It was like no one wanted to take the chance on a big promotion, and felt it was the safer option to recruit from outside—someone who had *been there, done that*. The evidence in the calibre of James's direct reports suggested that wasn't working out so well.

Simon talked her though the identification process for top talent at senior manager and director level. How this was translated, through discussion with the relevant executive into a succession plan for each role. Simon was fully aware of the limitations of that plan. He pointed to the repetition of the same three people as successors for senior roles and the number of senior roles that had *external hiring required* beside it. He knew it and she knew it, their succession was fragile and the document he showed her was really just words on paper. It was *box ticked*.

That put an onus on director and executive hiring. Lucy and Chris together had *ownership* of this activity, but in truth she knew that her stakeholders, the senior team, really would rather HR didn't get involved. There were exceptions, particularly when a piece of hiring was going off the rails and an executive was delighted to get Chris involved to ease the load. That was the exception. The majority of her peers and the top level of management were consistently non-compliant in their approach. They engaged with a headhunter they knew, before consulting any succession or talent list, and started putting *feelers* out in the market.

When they did go through the process of discussing with Chris or Simon what internal talent options there were, they were already set on the market. They *knew* that there was no one internally and were excited about getting in some *fresh blood*.

Chris had absolutely no objection to the use of headhunting firms for the senior hiring. After all it was still the most effective way of hiring senior staff. However, she was troubled that every search was a fresh start and they never built up any kind of market data or talent pools of senior candidates. She knew other businesses she had worked in had a longer-term senior hiring strategy. The issue was the immediacy of action in recruitment—it was only thought through when required. That and the fact that each director and executive used headhunting firms they knew personally and liked, as such there was a variation on approach for senior hiring.

Chris had quietly proposed with many of them that they work with a single supplier, or a couple of suppliers in order to create consistency and stability. They weren't wild about the idea but went along with her, reluctantly, and it was short-lived. In one instance, when she did convince an executive to work with one of the headhunters she felt would be best for the bank, he had also informed his favourites, who quietly and free of charge also did some approaches in the market. The executive felt this would help, but in reality, in a small market, it just made them look disorganised as some potential senior candidates were approached twice. Not at all good.

In the end Chris realised this wasn't a fight worth fighting and, as long as all the suppliers they wanted to use were approved by her and Lucy (which they all ended up being, to avoid unnecessary conflict) and they could monitor progress, she made no further efforts to control. After all, it was difficult to see a major problem.

What she did want to control, however, was the assessment for senior hires. It struck her as ridiculous that the branch staff went through a more robust process than people joining on six-figure salaries, with huge areas of responsibility. Typically, the headhunters would put forward two or three candidates, and the hiring manager would conduct an interview for a couple of hours. There was no common structure, and each exec had their own individual style, and immense confidence in their ability to pick great people. Usually they would ask a couple of their peers to also *have a chat* and the one piece of governance was that James, the CEO, would spend a half hour with the favoured candidate.

If there were no violent objections from the peer and CEO interviews, they moved to offer. It all seemed a bit hit-and-miss to Chris, and she was never sure they really had the best in leadership and technical strength at the top level. This would be a key point when she went back to James.

When they spoke about their combined findings, Lucy, Simon and Chris reflected on the story they had to tell. They shared the same thinking, and it was going to be a very difficult message. It wasn't that Lothian Bank never made any good or great hiring decisions. It wasn't that they didn't have rising stars through the organisation reach great heights. It wasn't that they didn't have people all over the business doing what they thought was best to fill their teams with the right people. The story they had to tell was of a business that didn't know it had a problem to solve in how it resourced people, and acted in the dark. There was little that was being done in HR or by the line managers that they could genuinely point to and say it was creating the uplift in capability that would propel the organisation into the future. They were busy doing the accepted things that merely had them treading water and not stretching forward.

Chris knew the discussion would be tough. However, she also knew that the first stage of fixing a problem was recognising it and no longer pretending that it wasn't there. That everything was just fine. She was excited because now they had acknowledged what the problems were, they could start to address them, and she had an ardent sense of purpose that this *could* all be fixed. It was fixable and it didn't mean reinventing the wheel. The little things, the attention to detail and a combined belief that this was the right thing to do would be a start. Beyond that, there was a lot they would achieve.

Hire Power

CHAPTER 7
REALISATION

"If you can't explain it to a six-year-old, you don't understand it well enough yourself."

Albert Einstein

By the time Chris and Lucy went into the meeting with James, they were fully aware of the grim story they had to tell. As they took him through the story it was clear that James was completely absorbed by their words—immersed and utterly engaged with what they had to say. He listened quietly and intently, only interrupting to ask questions a couple of times.

Chris knew James well, but it was still nerve-wracking to expose critical people strategy fault lines so openly. If anything, Lucy felt worse. She was new and yet she was describing a department that was struggling to contribute.

It became clear, however, that James's absolute attention wasn't because he was angry, or doubting, or blaming. He was absorbed because he saw potential in the picture they were portraying.

James knew immediately that their message said that, if the bank wasn't already sleepwalking into mediocrity it was certainly doing it's damnedest. It wasn't the fault of the people standing in front of him. He knew there was a collective dereliction of leadership. One that he would make sure was corrected. The answer lay with him, his team and the guys in HR collectively to get the organisation to wake up and address what was in front of them.

He listened to the realities of an HR function that had become reactive. He welcomed Chris's honesty about the way the different activities contributed to forcing HR into silos. He understood why the decisions and direction of each part of the mix sat separately, but he equally understood why this wasn't in Lothian Bank's best interest.

He was frustrated by the way that recruitment activity was given so little thought by the managers across the business. He was already very aware of the lack of progress with senior team building, as he saw that as being on him.

He now understood the issues quite clearly. They had no strategic plan for resourcing, they had poor execution throughout and there was no realisation that this was a problem, or that this was important. He realised they just let all this *stuff* happen. He knew that there wasn't any point in blame or attributing fault. Only now did he understand that the people who could change this and deliver the solution to the problems were overwhelmed by just keeping the wheel turning.

He listened to the problems with planning, the indifferent candidate experience, the poor succession plans and the lack of basic management capability in selection. He knew things would now change for the better. Chris and her team had done a great job in getting to the heart of all these problems and being so up front.

But how was a fix possible? It wasn't as if they could stop everything to remedy the situation. There would probably be a requirement from HR for expensive new technology. Wouldn't they also need a vast HR headcount expansion? Training for everyone? He knew Chris would have a solution, he just hoped it would be one that wouldn't create other issues.

Chris did have a solution. Lothian Bank would start making conscious decisions about the mix of resources it had, that it needed and how they would secure them. That could only be done by understanding what capability they needed, what did they need and then build a delivery plan for the gap. It wasn't complicated. They just hadn't done it before. They would ask themselves a simple question, "Do we have the capability to meet the long-term plan?"

They would conduct a capability analysis of every business unit and department. They would use the performance, talent and succession data they had as a starting point. They would then work with every one of the directors in the business to understand their capability needs against what the current state was. Build a big picture, and lots of little pictures. Then make decisions about *how*. They could no longer drift to a resourcing strategy.

Could each departmental head understand the departmental long-term plan and how that was related to the business long-term plan? Did they know what tasks and activity the realisation of that plan will create? Were they just figuring it out as they went along? Have they thought through what skills and capabilities they will need to deliver these tasks? Did they have the right skills to lead the team in the required direction?

Both Chris and James knew that some of the answers to these questions might pose some pretty tough talking points. The *what if...?* question loomed large in the room.

James was adamant though, this was the right thing to do. Chris was also aware that this was an opportunity for her department and team to deliver something for the business that would be tangible and meaningful. She knew that they should really be doing all this anyway.

Following the analysis there was a debate to be had about how they would build the capability for the future. Who are the successors? Where is the talent? Do we need to build or buy talent? Do we have a planned temporary and permanent mix? What is the strength of our early talent pipelines—does it work? Do we need more early talent, or less? Chris suggested that the gap analysis would pose the fundamental questions that would define how they would build the future. That would define what resources they required in HR, or how they would allocate the existing resources.

The final part of the plan was that they would need to weave this thinking and planning into the organisation for the long run. Chris was passionate about the possibilities for the organisation in not just solving some issues, but driving capability through informed thinking.

James also knew that whatever they decided he would then have a significant leadership role to play. There would need to be a shift in perception of how they resourced the business. It wasn't that the leadership team were trying to obstruct, or were neglectfully blundering through, it was just that they didn't know there was a problem. Addressing that would require an acceptance of the problem and a desire to change. Hearts and minds. Starting with his leadership team, and then their reports and all the way through the business, all the managers would have to get on board with the idea that resourcing their business with the right people was critical for the future. This was going to be a demonstration of his leadership and where he saw the priorities.

James gave the plan his full backing. He pushed them on delivery times, but assured them of his full support. They would talk to his executive team in their weekly meeting as soon as was possible. Chris would give regular updates on progress. And once the analysis was completed they would ensure the executive agreed the plan.

Nobody was in any doubt. This was important and they would make it work, and create a better and sustainable future. As Lucy left the meeting she realised with relief that not only did the CEO have confidence in her and had thanked her and Chris for their honesty, but that the future she was heading to was going to be very different. Hard work with high expectations, but she would have the chance to make a difference.

Chris realised that she had just committed herself and her team to a major piece of work, but she absolutely knew it was what the team should be doing. This was a game changer, and would be an ongoing focus. Chris and the team went to work and followed through as agreed with James.

James took the plan to the next leadership team meeting. He had little trouble convincing his executive that they needed to come along with this. They trusted him, and also knew that in one way or another they all struggled to get the right people. As the conversation with his team opened up, they all had severe concerns about capability, or their ability to get the future skills they needed. James had little time for those who took the opportunity to bash HR, or those who were defensive and pushed back on the exercise.

As they had proposed, Chris, Lucy and the HRBPs started with a simple organisation map and looked for gaps at director and senior management level. They then interrogated performance and potential data of the leaders in those areas from the talent data to build up a stronger picture. A good start, but they dug into the analysis through discussions with each of the executives about the directors and each of the directors about the senior managers—entirely focused on the capability and how that might work in the future. The HRBPs and Chris also had a view and contributed to the final picture. They produced a report for each area, which looked at current capability/short-term gaps and needs/long-term requirements. They had the bank-wide picture, and departmental ones.

It was not an easy exercise, but the information they gathered gave them what they needed. Some issues jumped right out as pan-bank themes and every department had short-term, as well as long-term capability issues that they could now address. Undertaking the exercise itself meant they were all having higher level conversations with their stakeholders.

Chris now knew the state of the staff and management at Lothian Bank better than ever before. Strengths and weaknesses. Issues and opportunities. Next was the plan to maximise the strengths, and minimise the weaknesses. Both Chris and Lucy felt a sense of satisfaction as it was clear that they were getting a real depth of insight. The business leaders had all come around and been honest and transparent as they understood that the motivation was in the long-term interest of the business. They were confident they would have a complete story to tell James when they went back to him.

They would need to shift attention from external recruitment to internal mobility. Their talent plan was ineffective and succession was a clear problem. They needed to focus activity on helping their most talented staff manage their careers in a way that kept them and benefited the business. They needed to quickly build successors for key areas. When they did recruit externally, they already knew how they did that would have to change completely. They also needed to address critical long-term skills needs, particularly for digital, and avoid duplication or competition internally from each area that would need these skills. They now also had a road map for each area of the business.

Lucy's expertise in understanding the external markets was also a major factor. When it came to defining the long-term strategy for resourcing this was central. No point in embarking on massive recruitment drives for skills that were in short supply. Or, if they were critical skills, they would have to understand the reality of the financial compromises that would be made. Every thorny recruitment issue involved a compromise. Better to plan and understand the compromises. It informed their thinking about what the resourcing focus needed to be. The plan to bridge the gap needed to be based in Lothian Bank reality and external market reality.

Chris also saw that the future of resourcing in Lothian Bank would need to change radically. They would move from the siloed approach that, she had come to recognise, created many of the problems and make sure that the resourcing plan rolled with the business plan. It would need visibility at the most senior level, accountability in HR and a strong message from James that he saw the resource plan as critical for the bank's success.

Chris knew there would be some investment required, but she also knew that there was a strong return on the investment. Whilst she recognised that James was forward-thinking enough to see that quality was the issue here, and that needed addressing, she wasn't naive enough to think that money would be thrown at the problem. Lucy had good ideas about how this could be funded. With some imagination and long-term thinking they would have to demonstrate a change in quality.

They would need to start over with the employer branding work. What it told them was next to useless and they needed to know what to promote externally and to staff as the real, exciting things about Lothian, and understand how to manage the downsides. That would be a priority. They would get an advertising communications supplier to kick that off.

The balance of temporary staff to permanent staff was something they needed to address. They were vulnerable in the contact centres, because they had constant turnover and low capability. They were also vulnerable in IT. Much of their technical capability was there on a contract basis. A massive risk, and one to address as a matter of urgency. Lucy's market knowledge revealed that these weren't all skills that were only available on the contract market. Many could be recruited permanently, with a well thought-through and resourced plan. A pleasant side effect of managing this issue would also be a significant financial saving.

They struggled to hire well and retain in head office. There were a couple of underlying problems. Firstly, they had a lack of internal mobility. Hiring managers weren't taking chances and people weren't applying internally. Easier to get a new role somewhere else. Chris was concerned that so much external hiring was disruptive and demoralising. They would always need to look externally for skills, and great people, but they had to start to shift the dial towards internal movement. Particularly at the first line manager level, where they would also need to ramp up training.

Lucy had highlighted the issue with head office recruitment. "Out of control," was how she had described it. Chris hadn't considered this a priority, but her view had now changed. Apart from the high spend, she hadn't previously seen a problem. She now realised that there were capability bald spots all over the business and horribly inconsistent line manager selection decisions. She trusted that, with more control and a budget to support, Lucy could drive consistency, reduce the spend and push quality upwards. It was a much more significant issue than anyone realised. They wouldn't ever want to take the selection decisions away from the mangers, but they needed to bring professional oversight to quality.

Aligned to the employer branding work, they planned to build communities of candidates for the critical skills they knew they would require for the future. They would move away from agency reliance and focus on nurturing the high calibre people they would need.

In the high-volume recruitment areas, a temporary staffing solution had been a sticking plaster on a large wound for some time. They realised they needed a full review. Start with the job analysis, change the candidate generation approach, look at assessment and start to manage onboarding through to induction and training. They would change the screening criteria to remove some of the barriers for good people and focus on quality in attitude and behaviours, use their existing technology better, introduce new tests, and streamline the assessment centre. The candidate was going to be the focus in their processes from then on.

They had fought with operations for years about capacity planning and how to control the numbers and Lucy had pointed out this was not going to be resolved. Better to ensure they have solid permanent recruitment flow, a pipeline for sudden uplift and keep the temporary supply available when required. Don't fix the planning problem, fix how you deal with it. Sally in operations was all on board, and Chris was confident this could be an early win.

If things were poor in the contact centres and head office, it was only by serendipity they even muddled through at executive level. The succession plans were a nonsense, and executive recruitment was a load of cosy chats. Some ropey decisions would have to be undone. A new focus for the talent team would be to zero in on successors for the director and executive roles. They would have to overcome the barrier of directors not releasing their best people easily. It was controversial, but Chris would suggest to James that the high-potential, high-performing talent cohort at senior manager level should be moved around. Some managers would have to let go of their best people and other managers would have to take risks in bringing them on. This would be centrally managed.

She knew she would get support for the final initiative. James loved the idea of graduates joining the business, after all that was how he started his career. But the leadership programme they currently offered was directionless. The graduates felt bumped from department to department, where they were treated as extra headcount and rarely given anything interesting to do. In conversation with one graduate she heard him say that the best thing about the graduate programme at Lothian Bank was that it was good to talk about in job interviews. That would need to change. In addition, they had identified the need to expand in areas that had no clear capability path and a market that couldn't be trusted to provide and sustain the level of skills they would need. So, for digital she would recommend that they start to grow their own talent and kick off a specialist digital graduate programme. There were other areas with the same problems, cybersecurity and risk jumped out, but that could wait.

Chris reflected on the work they had done, and was quietly satisfied. She, Lucy and Simon had opened up about the shortcomings in HR and how they had taken their eye off the resourcing ball. In a subtle way, they'd pointed out to James that he had as well, which he accepted. He was fully signed up to the process and whatever came from that. He would then know that change was necessary.

There was much to change, but all of it was achievable. There was nothing in their list that was beyond them. They knew the direction. They knew they needed a focus on Lucy's list of governance, capability and tools backed up by the leadership—with the cultural shift driven by James.

CHAPTER 8
THE THREE ESSENTIAL CONDITIONS

"By failing to prepare, you are preparing to fail."

Benjamin Franklin

When you talk to most people about their career paths, something about their journey becomes evident quite quickly. People move jobs regularly. Even those who have been with the same employer for twenty years will have held many different roles within the company. The traditional industries where someone joins, undertakes an apprenticeship and is then in the same job until retirement have been in sharp decline in Western economies for some years. Even where these industries thrive, increased automation is rendering these jobs redundant, and that single job for life is now recognised as belonging to a different time.

The average length of time someone stays with the same employer is five years in the UK. The average is four years in the US. That is according to 2017 research by the insurance company LV, and official US government statistics. In that time someone can expect, on average, just over one internal move or promotion.

This is of immense significance for organisations. It means that the entire capability of any business is fluid and changing. It means there are choices to be made.

There is risk in the fluidity, but also an opportunity. The risk is losing great people. The opportunity is control of the future. Everybody who moves on, or changes role creates a gap behind them. Individually each gap is a recruitment exercise. Across an entire business it's an opportunity.

The opportunity is the control to design and define organisational capability.

People will join and people will leave. Join in one role and move to another. Get promoted, join a newly created team, work in a project role. There may be a lot of the same faces around, but doing different things, have greater responsibility or change departments. This picture also just talks about people changing jobs. It doesn't reflect the changing nature of jobs in the modern workplace, account for roles that grow, or change through circumstances. Roles evolve quickly. People take on new responsibilities, but stay in the same job. It's all an opportunity to ensure the most capable people are doing the roles.

The modern organisation is a dynamic, shifting, morphing and reacting entity. It's almost like a living organism, which grows and repairs itself. The dynamism of the modern workplace presents an opportunity, but only if it is planned.

You have within your gift a chance to significantly impact the long-term capability of the organisation, as it moves through the regenerations. Impact positively, or impact negatively.

Put planning and strategy in place and as the organisation evolves there is the prize of shaping the evolution, building a sustainable and planned view of what organisational resource is. Building what you want it to be. Imagine the possibilities for changing and directing business capability and therefore business performance by using this flux to your advantage.

Seizing this future is taking a strategic approach to resourcing, and that can only happen when three fundamental conditions are in place.

There needs to be a long-term approach to *workforce planning*, linked to the business strategy. The plan only has value if the *execution and delivery is excellent*. Excellent delivery is only possible in a *culture* that values the activity and recognises the importance of resourcing. That culture can only thrive when there is a long-term approach to resourcing planning.

Individually, each of these conditions is important and will have some impact. It is *only* when all three are present that you have taken control of the design of organisational capability. With all conditions in place you can define the future you want.

THREE CONDITIONS—STRATEGIC PLANNING

A strategic workforce plan is the understanding and articulation of the direction of the enterprise, through people. It is the link between business performance and ambition and the skills and capability required to deliver that plan.

Understand what capability you will need to deliver the long-term plan. Understand what you have now. The gap informs your plan. Understand the external markets for the skills you need, what training is required and you give yourself the information to decide how to build. That's taking a strategic approach to planning. With this insight, you can then craft the priorities to deliver the capability. Recruitment, training, succession, early talent, contractors.

Knowing what priorities to focus on will be different for each organisation, and at the different stages of organisational development.

If the view of organisational capability is that you don't have the right people to deliver the long-term plan, you will want to ramp up external hiring. If the future is uncertain you might want to maintain a high level of temporary staff. If the market has skills shortages you may make location decisions, or design the roles differently, or start early talent pipelines and grow your own. It's about being informed.

The insight you gather in the strategic workforce plan should be used to design what the delivery of the capability is. You can control this. It will also change, so it is critical that once the culture of resourcing is in the right place, the strategic planning must become a part of the fabric and evolve over time to meet the changing direction. This will mean an operating model that is aligned to the plan, and therefore an operating model that may need to change, or have the flexibility to adjust with the plan.

THREE CONDITIONS—EXCELLENCE IN DELIVERY

Poor delivery renders the best plan worthless. Excellent delivery reinforces the value of planning and the value of resourcing.

Great delivery is completely dependent on the operating model. Make the decision about the shape of the operating model based on the long-term plan. Think carefully, what do all the contributing factors ultimately mean for how to deliver into the future? Will you need to do more external hiring or increase internal mobility? Build or recruit successors? Are there defined timed projects on the horizon? Have an operating model that reflects the priorities rather than a standard HR structure. Avoid silos, build flexibility. A good operating mode knits the parts of the mix together to address priorities. Having solid processes that complement each other and talk to the strategy.

At the heart of each one of those processes is an individual who will make a choice. Help them make the choice that works for you, and them. Processes need to fit around the individual and not the individual round the processes.

If you want to have good internal mobility, make it easy to look for jobs and encourage people to *feel* that it is a good thing to want to move on internally. They need to know that an approach to a manager to work in a different area will be welcomed. They need to know that their own manager will embrace a conversation about their career when it involves moving on somewhere else in the business. They need to know where to look, what they need to do to apply, what they need to be successful and that they will get the support. Feedback when they don't succeed and encouragement from their manager to build on the feedback for the next time.

If you want a vibrant internal jobs market, avoid commonly followed *don'ts*. Don't make it easier for the member of staff to apply externally than internally. Don't punish someone for trying and failing, so they want to leave. Don't ignore applications. Don't have someone in HR give the feedback. Don't make them ask their manager for permission to apply. Don't make internal notice periods punitive.

Having an internal job market is an easy thing to put in place. Jobs on the intranet, a policy that is sensible and a system that manages the movement. Turning the dial up and really making it something that makes the market dynamic takes cultural effort. Belief from the staff that there is a career path internally for them. Stories about success. Promotion of the intranet job board, internal careers fairs, and most importantly leadership and management sponsorship.

When it comes to the management of high talent in the business, the approach to centre around the individual must answer the *so what...?* question. The identification of talent needs to be consistent and have some objective. What individuals want from being on a high-potential, high-performing list is a career path that delivers their ambitions. Ambitions that tally with organisational needs. A list of high talent who are sent on great training courses, and have lots of learning and attendance at prestigious events may satisfy some, but that ultimately has little satisfaction for both individual and organisation. That satisfaction only comes with promotions, succession or valued lateral movement. A talent approach needs alignment to the movement of the individual.

There aren't many organisations that don't recognise the importance of the candidate experience for external hiring. A TMP Worldwide survey showed that 74% of employers completely agreed with the statement that, *the way a candidate is treated through the recruitment process will ultimately affect whether they want the job or not*. A further 23.3% slightly agreed. (Leaving a curious 2.7% who completely disagreed.) People know this is important, but the challenge comes with how that recognition is translated into action.

There is nothing in this that is tremendously difficult. Say what you are going to do, and then do it. Candidates want: communication, a timescale in recruitment that has been set out for them, an advertisement that they understand or an agency consultant who knows what they are talking about, assessment that relates to the role and is clearly fair, feedback when asked for, and more communication.

Again, there are many popular *don'ts*. Don't make the candidate feel like one more person going through your recruitment sausage machine. Don't let their application sit for weeks. Don't ignore the feedback request. Don't treat declined candidates like they just don't matter. Apart from the notion that they may be a customer someday, or already are, or might tell their friends, or apply later in their career when they are a star, they are a person. It's just not nice.

Too many organisations fail to understand that recruitment is a two-way street. The candidate (internal or external) is looking at you as much as you are looking at them. High-performing individuals will always have others to look at too. Don't assume that the balance is too heavily weighted in your favour. Be fair, transparent, honest and respectful. When things don't quite go to plan, tell them. Tell them what to expect. Give people notice. Fit the process to their timescales. Make them comfortable in interviews. That's what a candidate experience is. It's what you would want.

THREE CONDITIONS—CULTURE THAT EMBRACES RESOURCING

The notion that resourcing the business effectively is mission critical must be held at leadership level. It must permeate all management levels. Everyone who is responsible for filling a vacant position needs to be aware of the responsibility that carries. They all need to understand there are ways to improve the chances of getting it right, and there are ways to be a blind squirrel.

That may require a dramatic change in thinking.

A change in thinking about resourcing as a series of unconnected channels or activities. A change of thinking that recognises the constraints and barriers within the organisation that currently exist to stop strategic resourcing. A recognition that it really is the strength and capability of the people in the organisation that will create the competitive advantage. Recognise that impacting that is within your gift. Recognise that a focus on this is a winning plan, to be followed with determination.

An understanding that there is expertise in resourcing— employer branding, process management, assessment, candidate management, talent management, market insight, project management.

An organisation that has culturally embraced the importance of resourcing is Metro Bank in London. They have made planning and investment in resourcing core to organisational success.

As a challenger bank with a target of bucking the trend by providing banking services through a physical branch presence, they recognised the importance of getting the right people. Getting the right people and keeping the right people.

Right from the start the resourcing plan wasn't linked to an annual plan but to the rollout plan for the branch network. They built and revised the resourcing strategy based on the plan for the next twenty branch openings.

They developed a resourcing strategy that prioritised mobility for internal staff and looked for specific traits in new hires. There was real energy and action behind the drive for internal mobility. The CEO would personally host internal career fairs with the full support of the leadership team. Because of this clear message from the leadership there was no culture of stopping internal moves.

They assessed people for the traits that would survive and thrive in a changing and ambiguous environment, with a focus on customer service. The chief people officer (CPO) made the candidate experience the measure of success of the recruitment team rather than time or cost per hire. A focus on the inputs, rather than the outputs. They wanted the declined candidates to talk well of the experience and perhaps become a future customer, or *fan* as they are known in Metro.

They looked for *fluid intelligence* in their assessment and designed an assessment centre approach for the customer facing staff that measured the M factor. An assessment event that reflected the culture of the business, but was steeped in the need to measure characteristics that worked in the business.

It has worked for Metro. Ahead in the growth plan, and ahead in City expectations. The CEO and CPO recognise that this is because they have brought on the right people in the right way.

In an age when other banks steer away from the idea of physical presence banking, Metro drives towards that as underpinning the customer experience. When the customer experience is at the heart of a proposition, that right-people-in-place philosophy is core. They don't claim to have made every right decision in recruitment at senior or entry level, but they have given themselves the best opportunities to find the right people. And their approach and how they embrace the careers of staff is a fundamentally attractive part of their employer brand.

Yes, there are reasons why resourcing is so important. They are on a growth trajectory, so there is necessity in the resourcing investment. Without the people, the stores wouldn't open. But they have gone further. They have invested in resourcing, but anyone on a growth trajectory could do that. The difference is the culture in the bank. A culture that recognises the importance of getting the right people in, planning to that, planning to help people move and a leadership that embraces long-term career and resource planning. The leadership recognises the importance of resourcing, understands that there is expertise behind it and that enables the planning and execution.

There are many reasons why the three conditions are hard to find. It's easy to ignore problems that can't be seen. It's difficult to imagine the future. The trap of immediacy in recruitment delivery is easy. Doing what has always been done hasn't led to disaster. It seems difficult and the outcome is uncertain and in the distance.

Easier to fix problems as they emerge. It can feel like an investment on an HR initiative for no tangible return on investment.

The certainty is that thoughtful investment in securing the right resource for the business will reap rewards many times over. Every part of a business can call for greater attention and investment to realise benefits. Marketing to boost sales, operations to cut costs, design to make better products. Getting the resourcing mix right across all areas of the business with that focus on the capability will create long-term sustainable value in all areas. People really can be your biggest asset.

Hearts and minds. Strategic planning and insight. Excellence in execution.

Hire Power

CHAPTER 9
BUILDING A STRATEGIC PLAN

"Perfect is the enemy of good."

Voltaire

Do you have the capability to deliver the long-term plan? It's the simple question that is at the heart of strategic resourcing. What do you have, what will you need and how do you get it? It is a question of demand and supply.

There are many methods and approaches for developing a strategic workforce and capability plan. The right approach is organisation specific. It depends on the volatility of the business environment, the scarcity or otherwise of key skills, organisation strategic plan and so on. It can be straightforward if a business is in a steady state, or a real challenge if the future is uncertain. At times, the best to expect is an indicator of the direction of travel, rather than a description of the destination. It is essential to have a plan that looks towards a distant horizon.

There are basic principles that underpin the success of planning. It must be linked to the business plan, and revised as the business plan changes. It must be long term, ideally a minimum of three years. It must recognise the limitations of the internal and external market and therefore have the insight to mitigate those limitations. It needs to be flexible.

There needs to be clear linkage between the business leadership, ownership of the plan and execution of the plan. In other words, those executing the plan need to trust that the business leaders have completely bought into the plan and it is part of the business plan. Without that clarity, leadership and line management will doubt the validity of the plan.

The long view nature of the plan affords the time to develop internally, or brand build externally. It provides the succession pathways and gives clarity of direction for the development of talent. Long term gives that space for the build or buy, permanent or temporary choices to fulfil expectations.

The start of the plan is a gap analysis between what will be needed and what is currently in place. It's then supply and demand. The demand is the gap, and the supply is what exists already, what development of existing capability can achieve and what the market can provide.

Demand is framed by three questions—What? When? Where?

- **What** capability do we need to meet the long-term plan?
- **When** will we need those skills?
- **Where** will we need those skills?

Supply is what exists internally and what you need from the external market. Internal capability is the baseline with an evaluation of what the skills gap is for future demand, taking into consideration turnover, expansion, whatever training is in place, etc.

Understand what is in place currently and what the market will provide. This insight then informs your decisions about how to deliver. Knowing the supply doesn't exist, internally or in the local external market, gives you the opportunity to manage the problem in other ways.

With the plan developed you will then understand the *what*, the *where* and the *when*. Informing thinking for the *how*. Developing insight and challenging what the outputs mean for your organisation begins to make resourcing something that is consciously planned. This is taking control.

WHAT, WHEN AND WHERE.

The first insights you require to build the strategy are an appreciation of what you currently have and what you will need for the future. The understanding of what the current capability is sounds straightforward enough, but you need to be very clear what the critical criteria are by which this is judged. What level into the organisation does the analysis have to go? What do you do if you don't like the answer? What if there is a problem with capability in certain areas? Any efforts to increase organisational effectiveness through a resourcing strategy will also require robust performance management. Perhaps some tough decisions.

The very definition of current capability raises a couple of questions. What does the performance management process tell about capability? Is there a talent mapping of performance and potential? You may feel that these existing tools already provide the information that you require and as such you have a good feel for what the organisation capability already is. There are warnings with that assumption. Existing data is an obvious and valid starting point, it may not provide you with the level of information that you will need.

Firstly, the performance management process will inevitably be a comparative process. By design or by default the performance of high, medium and low performers across the business will be a normal distribution or bell curve. So, an absolute faith in this measure as an indicator of overall business capability will be limited to cross-company comparison. In reality, that may even be limited, as the normal distribution will be applied to all large populations within any substantial business.

This means the comparative performance/capability can just be applied within groups, not even the entire organisation, or the possibilities of the external world. Some organisations force a normal distribution on performance and others allow a freer hand for the awarding managers. Either way the impact is broadly similar—performance over a large population will be viewed as good, bad and average in a statistically similar way. If you intend to shift what *average* is, then changes will be required.

Secondly, although we want insight about current capability the whole purpose of the exercise is to understand what opportunities or threats the existing capability presents for the future. Performance management is, by definition, a retrospective measure and indicates how someone has done, not what they are capable of. It also doesn't identify capacity to adjust or grow.

However, that's where the talent measure of potential comes in. Yes, this is a future looking tool and should identify the brightest and the best in an organisation. The problem with talent management processes however, is that they are often in the hands of managers who view it as an HR process to be got through, an exercise in amateur psychology, or an opportunity to reward favourites. Regardless of how good the tools are, the point is that it is subjective and implemented with variable enthusiasm. The measurement of potential is even more subjective.

The combined outcome is that high performance and high potential yardsticks are different across the organisation. They also may not be any indicator of what is needed in the future, and if the entire organisation has a capability issue the relativity of the tools will not provide any indication that much external refreshment is required.

The purpose of pulling this picture together is to build the baseline to understand the capability gaps that will need plugged if the business wants to meet the long-term objectives. Choose the parameters that are relevant to you. What level of management to take the exercise to? What scale? How detailed? Purely on skills or also on behaviours?

The next thing is to look at what will be needed in the future. Understand what the plan says, understand what tasks and activities need delivered to meet the plan. The tasks will point to the skills that will be required. This is not an exercise in building an organisation chart of the business three years out, but an exercise in gathering insight into what each area of the business will require. The leader of each business should know what they will need, and how that contributes to the plan. Broad strokes and principles are good enough for the future.

The secret with understanding future capability requirements is translating what the long-term business plan is likely to mean in terms of the activities that will require getting done. Keeping it simple helps. There is a business plan that will talk to every part of the business. It is not a massive leap from understanding what you will be required to do, to knowing what skills you will require your staff to possess. Therefore, you can look at each department relatively far out and have a feel for what they are likely to need.

However imperfect or imprecise they are, these processes will give you the gap analysis of where you are to where you want to be. That will then throw up the questions about how to bridge the gap. That can only be addressed with insight of the external market part of the supply mix. Knowledge of what the market can provide and how the market is changing informs the decision as to how you can go deliver.

The very fact that you are looking three-plus years out means that you can make decisions now that will yield benefit in the short, medium and long term. If you know that certain skills are scarce in the organisation, but will be vital, you have the time to build a proposition and an attraction strategy to generate interest with the population who have those skills. Even if you don't know the precise roles. If you know that the market is particularly tight for certain skills, you at least understand that you need to build the training, or bring in graduates or apprentices. If the talent for rare skills command salaries and that market is outside your pay policy, at least you understand that before it becomes a problem and you can make informed decisions about your reward approach.

Develop a deep understanding of external employment markets and the skills environment that you rely on. This knowledge informs your decisions as to what are the skills you can buy in, or grow them yourself. What is available in the permanent recruitment market, and what is available on a contract basis? Of course, the answer is a combination of approaches, but this guides the decision on the balance. You will need insight into the limitations of your markets, what the opportunities are, how they are changing, and where are the emerging skills being developed that you will need.

The Commonwealth Games in Glasgow in 2014 was a tremendous success. Most events sold out and the Scottish public rallied around the games. For the first week, even the sun shone! The success of the games would have been impossible without the recruitment of the 1,600 people required to put a major event together.

What it provides is an example of what a strategic workforce plan can enable. Working with limited resource (such as only having four interview rooms) the recruitment team knew that resource and budget were going to always be tight. Planning was key. They started eighteen months in advance.

That meant that they planned every detail of what they needed to do with precision and could account for the limit on resource. Of course, it didn't help that before they even started the plan was ripped up and they had to start over, with the requirement then rising from 1,300 to 1,600. But the planning template was in place, and they absorbed the changes.

Even with the pressure on to meet every hire, the team was also able to meet quality and diversity objectives. As they had the long-range knowledge of what roles they needed to fill they could select the source channels well in advance for candidate generation.

They utilised the services of organisations like Remploy, who find employment for the local disabled workforce, making sure that diversity was a key part of the strategy from the outset. In addition, part of the core purpose of any major games event is to create a legacy. This was achieved by helping people on relevant degree courses work on a project that was a unique opportunity on their doorstep. The recruitment team achieved this by working closely with Scottish universities.

At the heart of all these global major events, there sits strategic workforce planning and a drive for high-quality recruitment delivery.

Who thinks of strategic resource planning, however, as they watch the great sporting drama unfold?

Delivering recruitment for the Commonwealth Games was a one-off exercise. It isn't a single event for other organisations. Whatever way the strategic workforce and capability plan is compiled, it needs regular calibration with the business plan. Regular review and updating. The first time will always be the most difficult. From then onwards, there is never the build from a blank sheet again, plus there is the demonstration of the value of the process. Value that is only realised with excellent execution, and that starts with a way of delivering—an operating model.

HOW

Knowing the demand and understanding where the supply comes from informs the thinking on the requirements to bridge that gap. Are there any critical gaps? Do you need entry talent programmes? Temporary or permanent? Can you grow your own capability? What external hiring is required? Now you have the insight to answer the questions.

Delivering the plan will always be subject to constraints of resource. Not only does the insight in planning reveal what the gaps are, it guides allocation of whatever resource is available. Informed choices can be made about the priorities. Training. Talent. Recruitment.

The tobacco industry provides examples of operating models that are shaped to meet the plan, and the environment. They have needed to react to changing public attitudes to the industry.

With certain jobseeker market segments, notably the younger generations, tobacco is not on their career radar. Corporate social responsibility has become increasingly important as a differentiator in the last twenty years and the tobacco industry has a tough sell to that generation.

This is not lost on the people who manage resourcing in the industry. They have made conscious resourcing decisions based on this awareness. Firstly, they know they need to pay above market, and are willing to do so. They also make sure that their senior reward propositions reflect loyalty. They will offer a graduate proposition that puts them on a par with the investment banks. However, that is not sustainable if the graduates leave after two years and they experience high turnover throughout.

The reality is tobacco businesses have low turnover in comparison with similar manufacturing industries. One major contributing factor to this is that because they anticipate external hiring pressure the big companies in the sector make a huge effort in creating and maintaining an internal jobs market that enables staff to have long and varied careers in the one business.

Career planning is part of management conversations, moves are encouraged, risks are taken, and tobacco companies generally encourage relocation with more than just a financial incentive. Faced with the reality of a potentially alienated external market these businesses have made conscious decisions to ensure that they create great career paths for their good people.

An operating model is dependent on so many factors, more than just the balance of supply and demand and the conclusions of how to bridge. The capability to deliver the pan is also critical. Capability of managers and capability of HR. No point in designing an operating model that will fall over because it's too complex or makes demands people cannot or will not meet.

It may mean a change for some in HR, particularly talent management and resourcing activities. The resourcing capability discussion isn't just a critique of the capability of the people in HR, but an overall appraisal and understanding of how the whole organisation approaches and executes resourcing. From resource planning, through temporary staff governance, policy, talent identification to recruitment and within that the competence and responsibilities of everyone in the process.

Many organisations have driven through huge resourcing change programmes without the full engagement of managers in the business. This leads frequently to a further disconnect between the users of the hiring service (i.e. managers with the need) and the delivery recruitment teams. It has almost invariably been the case that the driver for change was cost reduction. Often the results were the unintended consequence of damaging the quality of hiring, and further damaging the perception of HR.

In the end a focus on quality and the improvements in execution through better thinking and planning will be a cost saving. Keeping quality as the goal is a much better way to get there. (A better way, but a more sophisticated business case to build. The saving isn't the annual straight-line reduction of a resourcing budget.)

However, the truth of the matter is that an effective resourcing operating model is not about building a massive and costly resourcing structure. Far from it.

Most of the changes that organisations need to make to improve the way they attract and retain the talent that they will need are adjustments in thought, or execution of what is already in place. Joining-up, shifting emphasis, better communication, sharper practice and a consistent and understood message about what the purpose is and why the resourcing *mission* is so critical.

For the operating model to succeed it's this culture of common purpose and intent, when it comes to doing things right on resourcing, that is important. It requires an understanding of how all the elements of the resourcing mix fit together, or don't, and how effective each part is. Silos will blunt the purpose. There needs to be a whole view of the resourcing mix, not isolated single lens views. The right governance, supported by the right tools appropriate for the capability.

There is a long list of governance considerations, such as a policy for internal movement. Is promotion a local decision, based on time served, or part of a talent programme? What is the policy to define when external recruitment can commence? What is the policy of internal candidates and external candidates both applying for the same role? Is there a policy for screening? An operating model needs rules and clear responsibilities to work effectively, like a policy framework.

If resourcing isn't considered a strategic driver, it is likely that sensible policies meet legal and ethical requirements, but don't necessarily have a capability impact. A successful operating model will start with the principles of delivery that the plan directs and answer the questions in detail. The policy should tie to the principles and support the execution.

When it comes to delivery, regardless of the balance of activity, success is dependent on everyone knowing their role and being equipped to perform that role. Not a melange of stuff carried out in a happy-amateur way. Whether that is enshrined in a policy, code of practice or inscribed on velum parchment is irrelevant. What is very important is that it is clear to all, and that they buy into their roles. An operating model will struggle without that.

The right tools to do the job are therefore an essential. They are not, however, the silver bullet answer. Many organisations will look for a technology solution that fixes any recruitment woes. A new applicant tracking system has often been implemented on the back of a massive cost saving projection that is based on a misunderstanding that it is the strategic answer. It is not—it is a tool of the job.

The tools are important. The right tools make the job simpler. Rather, the right tools in the right hands, used the right way make the job simpler. And new technologies to help manage talent, screen applicants, assess applicants and manage candidate communities are emerging every day.

PLANNING AND CULTURE

Having the plan is great, but if the culture is set against resourcing progress, then it just won't work. We have seen that recruitment or resourcing and much of the surrounding agenda hasn't typically been considered of the highest value. We know this creates problems, and misses opportunities.

We also know that businesses have multiple agendas, and human resources has a long to-do list. However, it should not be a difficult sell to the business leadership that planning to improve the capability and reduce gaps in workforce through the adoption of a resourcing strategy will only be a good thing. The most important element of any shift to strategic resourcing is that they not only understand this, but have the culture to support the strategy.

Consultancy A is an American consulting financial services firm. Consulting is one of those industries where the need for smart recruitment and staff development is widely recognised, because there is a clear straight-line link between consultant capability and revenue, which sharpens the motivation for thinking strategically about resourcing. What Consultancy A has done is a great example of how the planning and culture of strategic resourcing coming from the top, produces a change in approach. They are getting the subsequent results.

The firm had a very clear plan of what size they wanted to be and the markets from which they expected to generate the growth by sector and geography. Talent management and recruitment accountability sit with one person, separate from the HR function and that individual reports directly to the CEO. To him the idea of a resourcing strategy was something so important he wanted a direct report to have total oversight and ownership of the plan.

The CEO is fully aware that delivery of the plan is entirely dependent on having the right skills and expertise in place in the right markets. He combined talent and recruitment functions under one director and had him report directly to him, out of the normal HR reporting line. This wasn't a reflection on other capability, but a recognition that getting resource in place warranted his absolute attention.

They operate to a three-year plan of talent moves, backfill hiring at more junior levels and experienced hiring when required. Where they have enjoyed success is that they have this long-term talent plan linked to the growth strategy and know in advance where they will require external hiring. With this in mind, the plan enables the head of resourcing and talent to actively map external talent in the specific geographies and sectors and build the external network of likely new hires well in advance of the need to hire, because they knew where these gaps were likely to be.

This enables them to plot a specific direction and make informed decisions based on available talent. Furthermore, they check progress of the plan against a financial plan and make a simple correlation between the talent/resourcing strategy and the growth of the business.

Professional consultancy, where there is a straight-line billing ratio to individual competency is a very straightforward example of the working of the principles, but it's completely intuitive to understand that it's transferable to all industries, sectors and organisations.

The consultancy firm in the example has answered the capability questions and developed their operating model. They know where they are, where they are going, their internal and external markets and have the structure to manage what they need to do. What they had above all of that though, was an absolute endorsement from the business leadership that this was a business-critical activity.

Being aware that there are problems in an organisation that have a resourcing root, or that there are missed opportunities because there simply isn't the right capability is precisely the right starting point. However, that realisation may just present a problem about how to resource the business that seems like a mountain too steep to climb. The answer to the question, "Do we have the right capability to meet our long-term plan?" may yield deeply uncomfortable answers.

It is then tempting to fixate on sticking plaster solutions, and address tactical issues in isolation from the consequences or the ultimate objective. The ultimate objective is to have the right people, doing the right things, in the right place at the right time. *What, where, when* and then you can focus on the *how*.

Break the problem down and develop a deep understanding of what the challenge to be tackled is. At this point you can make informed decisions about what you want the focus to be. Supply and demand. Look to the long term and understand what needs delivered. The clever part is then using that information to inform how you intend to deliver.

That decision is choosing to move the resourcing future from one of accident and chance to one of control over your resourcing destiny. Making informed decisions about how increases your chances of getting better quality staff doing what you want more often.

It then requires excellence in execution, or the planning is as good as pointless.

Hire Power

CHAPTER 10
MARKETING STRATEGY

"Why McJobs are bad for your kids"

Washington Post headline, 1986

There is an old joke in recruitment about the HR manager who died and, being an honest and caring HR professional, was immediately transported up to heaven. When she arrived at the pearly gates, St Peter informed her that before deciding on her eternal resting place, she would need to look at both options. Heaven and hell.

"Ah, OK, sounds fair..." replied our recently deceased HR manager and jumped in the lift off down to hell. Naturally she had low expectations, but when she arrived, she was stunned by what she encountered. Beelzebub himself answered the door, dressed in a Hawaiian shirt and beach shorts. He smiled broadly and merrily ushered her inside. She was astonished to see a fantastic beach party, with live music, lots of cool (dead) celebrities, great food and amazing looking cocktails.

Later in the day she played a great round of golf in the hell recreation of Pebble Beach, and relaxed at a BBQ afterwards. She thanked everyone for their time and went off back up the lift for the heaven tour.

That was also great, but in a different way. Lots of angels on clouds and a fair amount of pleasant harp playing.

Back at the pearly gates she pondered her decision.

"Well, where do you want to spend all eternity?" St Peter asked.

"Well..." she said, not wishing to offend, "heaven was great, but hell seems just a bit more, well, sort of, *me*..."

So, St Paul thanked her for her time and she was taken straight back down to hell. The devil once again opened the door. As it opened she cast her eye behind him over a scene of misery and pain as the inhabitants pushed large boulders around a fiery, barren landscape. As they strained against the massive rocks these miserable wretches were constantly whipped by cackling demons.

"What..." she stammered, "is this?"

"Well," replied the devil, "yesterday you were a candidate, and today you are staff."

THE EMPLOYER BRAND

The principles of effective resourcing execution are universal, regardless of any distinctions between internal, external, entry-level or executive. You need to find qualified people who want to do the job, find out if they are right for it and move the best person into the role. Attract, assesses and onboard. At its most basic this is something we ought not to overcomplicate.

Keep the process simple. Use technology where you can. Keep the human touch where you should. Make sure people know what they are doing. Make the process easy for the user, personal for the candidate. Make promises, and keep them. Be fair, be searching, be thorough. Use the experience of the individual and insight from data to make informed decisions. Have a plan. Have a plan B.

Attraction falls into two separate elements. Firstly, there is the branding you have as an employer, and how you use that for your benefit: to be recognised as a destination for specialists who work in your industry, an employer who people aspire to work for, a unique, compelling identity as an employer. Establishing how you can use your employer brand sets the framework for the external market, and in no small way lets your existing employees feel an attachment, a pride, and a reminder of what is good about the place.

The second part is moving from the aspirational feelings created by the employer brand and translating that into applications and great hiring. Converting all those warmed-up prospects into real staff who contribute. This is a completely different challenge, but one that requires a great deal of thoughtfulness. There are multiple channels for the candidates to filter through to you. Understanding where to get the best ones, how to spend the budget wisely and how to manage all the different channels, requires insight and a deep understanding of the markets and the candidates in those markets.

The employer brand, and EVP, is what people internally and externally think about what it means to work for your organisation. It's a very real thing, and you have one whether you know it or not, or have attempted to manipulate it or not.

Jeff Bezos, the founder of Amazon, said, "Your brand is what people say about you when you are not in the room."

That applies to consumer brand, product brand, personal brand and employer brand. What is it really like to work there? To expand Bezos' sentiment, you could say that your employment brand is what your staff say about you to their friends in the pub after a tough day in the office. More likely and more wide reaching is that now, they are just as likely to say it to 200-plus of their closest friends through social media. It is a new reality that in the world of twenty-first century employment, not only do employees and potential employees have opinions about the sort of environment that they want to work in, those opinions will be based on multiple sources of evidence. Good people will make choices based on that reality, to join, to stay, to not apply or to leave.

The emergence of websites like *Glassdoor* take talking with people in the pub about where they work and make it a comparison website, a sort of TripAdvisor for jobs. This makes the case for understanding your employer brand even more compelling. The evolution has moved from conversations with friends, to the wider social media conversations, to global public domain opinions. This isn't a trend that is going to reverse. Understanding your employer brand and making the conscious decision about how to use that information is something that cannot be avoided.

There are a couple of uncomfortable realities here. Firstly, and most significantly, is the idea that the opinions people have about working for your firm will be largely based in fact. That means that if your business has a working environment like a Victorian poor house, then presenting it like there is free beer and sunshine will only work for a short time. If you deceive anyone into joining, they are unlikely to hang around for long. People will make choices to leave and, although you may be able to recruit replacements through deceptive marketing, there is nothing as potent as mismatched promises to encourage short-term tenure in your business. The reality is that if your employer brand is toxic, you actually have much bigger problems than recruitment.

Even if the perception of candidates is not based in fact, even if there is a gross misrepresentation about your organisation, perception is king with branding. You have to deal with that and manage accordingly.

The second uncomfortable truth is that often events outside your control can impact your employer brand. Take the sudden emergence of the expression *McJob*, which was first coined by the Washington Post in 1986. To put it mildly, this has not been helpful for McDonald's. The term is used to describe a job which is dull and with no prospects of advancement. At the time of going to press this was almost certainly the case in the fast food industry.

McDonald's have refuted the slur, but the concept has stuck to the point of inclusion in the Oxford English Dictionary. McDonald's will tell a tale of employee engagement, structured management paths, career opportunities, first-class training and so on. However, their organisation has become synonymous with a deeply pejorative term for low-wage, low-prospects employment.

If you don't understand what your existing employer brand is, if you don't understand what people are saying about you, then you cannot possibly start to control that and thereby talk to the right people in the right way. Control does not mean portraying a false message, that just creates further problems. Employer branding is a subtle business. Getting the balance right between telling the truth and painting a positive picture is the key.

Balancing the employer brand message is a bit like using a graphic equaliser on an old hi-fi system (if you remember such things). The music doesn't change, but what you can do with the dials is adjust the outputs so that you can accentuate the sound to your preference. Make it sound as good as it can. Increase the amount of bass or treble. If someone doesn't like classical music to start with, it's unlikely they ever will, but the adjustments present the format at its very best.

In employer branding work the subtlety is in accentuating the most positive aspects of working at the organisation. Either the brand is already imprinted with the candidate market you are talking to, in which case you are drawing attention to the bits that you want them to focus on, or it's all new. In that case you are setting the first impression as a favourable one.

So, what measures can be taken to develop and communicate what you want as an employer brand? Understand what the brand means, what you want it to mean and carefully choose the channels and ways of communicating the message.

UNDERSTANDING THE BRAND

The first thing to do is to establish what the current state is. Gather information from all available data sources on what the organisation is like to work for and what people externally think it is like. Perceptions and realities.

A staff opinion survey is a good place to start, but it doesn't tell the whole story. For a start, the employee opinion survey catches a moment in time, and as such the results can be skewed to reflect short-term impacts. The best employer brands describe clearly what the core of an enterprise stands for, and that is not a transient message. An employee opinion survey is great for that initial check, but insight requires greater depth.

A great way (unsurprisingly enough) to understand what it's like to work in your business is to ask the people who work there. Structured focus groups draw out the story underneath the findings in the employee opinion survey. If run by a good facilitator who is considered neutral by the attendees, these can yield a great deal of insight about working life—the surprising things that people love about the business and the ugly things that drag them down. The key is to pick between the delights and gripes about their individual situation or individual managers and identify which are institutional plusses and negatives. For example:

- What makes them proud to work there?
- What do they like?
- What frustrates them?
- How do they describe the environment to their friends?

Focus groups will also highlight the differences between locations and business areas. The front-line staff experience of working for you may be totally different from that of head office staff. Senior management from entry-level. It will also differ from location to location, and country to country. All valuable insights, and these differences pose interesting questions when it comes to deployment.

You will also need the view of the leadership of the business. What do they think it is like working in the business? This will be a more optimistic view of the organisation than staff, but it is an essential part of the mix. This also often serves as the aspirational view of what they want the business to be. Disparities between what their view is and the feedback from the staff they lead creates the debate as to what the message really should be. Balance.

The final part of the 360 view is the external view. That is the view of people from the candidate populations and markets that you might like to come and work for you. Is their perception of what the working environment is like any different from what employees say? The external view is possible to listen to through online surveys on careers websites, however that will only provide a small and self-selecting sample that could be hopelessly wrong. Again, the best way is in location or specialist-specific focus groups. This is an important group to hear from, and accuracy of output is best achieved by a third party. It's worth the expense to get the view.

In all aspects of the data and insight gathering what you want is truth. As difficult or as delightful as it is. No point in self-deception. Whatever the negatives are you need to know—to work to rectify, manage through the process or openly raise with candidates as they get to the final stages.

Tesco Bank provides a good example of variations in employer brand that can exist in the same organisation.

It was founded in 1996, as a joint venture between RBS and Tesco. In 2007, it was wholly bought by Tesco. The year after, as they were embarking on their growth drive, came the financial crash. A crash which had RBS at the epicentre in the UK.

This presented an interesting branding challenge for the recruitment team there. Their task was to take the business from a handful to approximately 5,000 in about three years. The first big push was in customer services and they launched a project to develop the employer brand.

With their advertising supplier, they conducted many external focus groups. Internal focus groups or staff surveys were not possible as there were too few staff and none of them yet worked in a customer facing role.

They did however, establish a very clear impression from both the bank leadership and Tesco leadership as to what the new bank would stand for. It was going to be different in the market, and not fall into the habits of the established banks, who thrived on exploiting customer inertia. The customer would be at the heart of the bank, as it was in the supermarket business.

The focus group outputs threw up a couple of interesting outcomes. Firstly, the message really resonated with candidates. Many were ex-financial services and had been really jaundiced by their experiences during the crash. It had been an unpleasant time to work in financial services. The other thing that really resonated was the idea that it was Tesco. Neither the recruitment team, nor the advertising agency were sure if the supermarket brand would chime in a financial services market, but the environment dictated that it was *the* key selling point for people joining in customer service roles.

From that output, the campaign *Fresh Careers at Tesco Bank* was born, playing on the retail history of Tesco with food imagery in the advertising and reflecting the newness of the enterprise. The whole strategy for volume recruitment was to lean heavily on the parent brand.

Some time later they wanted to revamp the employer brand messaging for head office. They found that for head office staff, almost universally banking professional staff coming from large competitors, the parent brand, a supermarket chain, had less appeal. Less appeal to the point that it often wasn't seen as a smart career move with a future. The employer branding approach for head office was therefore completely different, and talked to the career opportunities of joining a smaller firm. The chance to have greater freedom and a chance to grow skills. *Grow with us* became the head office employer branding campaign. Not a banana to be seen.

Both campaigns promoted the truth. The parent company did provide the security and feel that the customer service staff responded so well to. The scale of the bank did give head office staff personal growth opportunities and scope on the role. The campaigns' success came from focusing the most attractive message to the appropriate market.

The information and insight you get forms the basis of what you want the output of the employer branding message to be. You need to find the themes, both positive and negative. Positive as the ones to promote, but the negative things that come out should also give you food for thought. How do you manage those realities?

As an example, if a business brand is slow moving, bureaucratic and difficult to get things done, then just how does it deal with candidates who thrive best in fast-moving environments? The business may well want and need that very type of person, and the candidate may well think they can overcome the internal hurdles, but is this just a recipe for a short and difficult relationship?

Or you have a high-pressure, very intense working environment, which may reward well, but can also burn people out quickly. Understanding what your business is really like and then understanding the candidate against that backdrop at least enables you to make an informed decision. Clarity of employer brand should also enable the candidate to make an informed decision. If the decision is, "Not for me!" that is a good outcome.

The output from the collection of themes should be agreement as to what the organisation stands for and what messages you want to put out there. Honest, but positive. Messages that are easy to understand for those outside the organisation, recognisable as life inside by staff. This may be a difficult square to circle. Every workplace throws up frustrations that become burdensome to people over time, particularly at the front line. By the very nature of these roles and the high-volume areas these will take up a great deal of effort for recruitment and the markets here will be the targets of the EVP. The positive message you portray externally will not chime with all internally all the time. Again, balance.

You now have an employer brand that you understand and have some control of. So how do you use it?

EMPLOYER BRAND DEPLOYMENT

Employer branding is a strategic exercise for human resources, but it's use is all too often tactical. Internally it will perhaps define a new look and feel to corporate communications, but might not reflect the reality of the culture. A *new* employer brand certainly won't create organisational change. It's a mirror, not a catalyst.

To maximise the value of your employer branding work externally it should be used to speak to the markets you want to develop interest in the organisation over time. Good employer branding is not a nice new colour palette for advertisements, or a collection of great straplines. It is a long-term, interest generating tool.

What tends to happen is that the branding is used in an advert for specific jobs, rather than to create an overall impression of working in that organisation. The very point of a brand is to create that fuzzy feeling about the product (in this case a job) that eventually pulls you to it when you are in the market. If the jobseekers see the output of your branding exercise only once, and that is in the job that they have applied for, then the branding hasn't done the intended job. It's simply made the advert nicer.

That approach reflects the product of much of the output of employer branding. They stick to specific hiring projects. As the CEO of the UK's largest recruitment communications business puts it, "The money follows the vacancy."

BMW don't expect to sell a car from a TV advertisement, or from an advertisement in an airplane magazine. What they expect from their advertising is to create that feeling in their target markets about the life they could have with a BMW. Then, when that person is looking to change car, or wants a prestige brand, or reaches the stage in their life where they want to show their success off, the BMW hope is that they already feel excited about their brand. They don't expect someone to pick up a magazine on the red-eye and call them on landing to place an order.

Yet in recruitment that is almost precisely what we expect to happen, if the branding is only attached to individual jobs. A jobseeker searches for jobs online, or looks in the paper and sees your advertisement alongside other, similar advertisements and applies. That is then the entirety of their brand experience. All the good work in building a clever brand proposition and EVP is rather wasted.

That sounds an expensive waste of time and effort.

It is expensive. Advertising in recruitment is not a cheap business and that is why you want to get value for the money. What is more expensive? Embarking on a branding exercise in target markets and building that long-term fuzzy feeling for your business, or spending on advertising each individual role, using agencies when that fails and having the *money follow the vacancy*?

If the long-term planning is inaccurate then the strategic option runs the risk of being upfront investment for no return. If you trust the planning, the first is the more cost-effective route, but more difficult to quantify and justify as the benefits are not on a per-vacancy basis. And, fundamentally the reason you build the brand in the first place is to attract the right people for your organisation. The best people for your organisation. It is tied up with quality and capability. So, it's frustrating when the employer branding work becomes a tactical tool.

That's back to the need for all the critical aspects of strategic resourcing to be in place. An understanding and trust at business leadership level as to the need for and benefits of long-term strategy in resourcing will enable the strategic use of the brand. Trust in the long-term workforce plan makes the best approach the cost-effective approach. With these in place the brand messaging can be deployed with confidence through advertising, online campaigns, public relations exercises and so on.

There is sense in building the brand to make candidate generation much more cost-effective. There are many other reasons. The creation of a positive first impression will give you an edge over the competition. A great brand will have the candidate excited when they start (all of course, if backed up through the process, but we'll come to that). So, there are huge positive cost and quality impacts.

There is a further compelling advantage when building a recruitment brand and creating candidate communities. One of the tactical issues that organisations face and will always face, regardless of the intention or accuracy of the long-term plan, is fluctuation in short-term numbers required, or the need to recruit for leavers at short notice. When you have created a community of candidates that are interested in the organisation there is a much greater chance of being able to switch on the tap quickly. Preventing the starting-from-scratch approach every time, reduces the pressure on recruitment and has an upward effect on quality, and downward on cost.

The only reasons not to build an employer brand that isn't attached to an identifiable vacancy is if you don't trust the plan, or you think you'll never recruit again.

How you deploy the overarching branding message most effectively is down to organisation, circumstances and opportunity. It is an ongoing set of messages. Community building and reinforcement. Advertising, public relations, events, online presence, blogs, stories. All with a consistent, positive message. All that create interest in the organisation, the careers page on the website and eventually a role.

GCHQ, Government Communications Headquarters, required people to work in Cheltenham in their cybersecurity division, responsible for protecting UK assets. The market for these skills is narrow, and traditional advertising is not something that has typically been effective in generating a response for roles.

The advertising agency tasked with the solution realised they needed to get to the target group, challenge their thinking and inspire them to be *activated*. They created a challenge in the form of a code that was seeded in blog environments frequented by individuals with potential cyber skills.

Those who successfully cracked the code had a *reveal* of the role of cybersecurity specialists in GCHQ. It was suitably complex to stimulate the technical interest in the community, acted as a first-level screen, and generated interest. With viral pushing of the campaign through the communities and the PR impact of the approach, they generated 2.2 million unique visitors to the website.

TURNING THE COMMUNITY INTO APPLICATIONS

Hiring requires a tactical deployment of the brand and an understanding of the recruitment channels you have at your disposal and which candidates will come to you through which channels.

Recruitment markets are constantly changing and defining them isn't a precise science. There are many parallels with consumer marketing and there is much in the way of sophistication that recruitment marketing can learn from marketing, particularly when it comes to market insight. Technology and the pace of modern life has altered markets dramatically in recent years. They can exist by geography, specialism, experience and skills or a combination of all these factors. Where consumer marketing looks to segment its customers, working with candidate markets also requires segmentation, but segmentation that is more meaningful than generation X stereotypes, generation Y or millennials. Insight in the market yields an appreciation of subtlety and sophistication that broad chronological labels miss.

What product marketing professionals understand so well, is the behaviour of their customers. They tailor products to meet customer segments. Marks and Spencer didn't develop the *meal for two for a tenner* concept on a whim. They understand that there is a customer segment that has a behaviour pattern that fits the product and the price point. They know their customers.

Correctly deployed, the employer branding message will create a favourable impression of your business with the markets you need to be talking to. This is aligned to the strategic workforce and capability planning that you have done. You will be making the organisation attractive to the skill areas that, at some stage, there will be vacancies for. That will still require a tactical deployment at the point of need, but it is a different proposition from a cold start if there is already warmth towards your brand.

As the company expands with the plan, or as the roles appear, this warm and fuzzy feeling that you have generated needs to be translated into a discussion, assessment, offer and joining. The key here is to have insight into the particular markets you are interested in and then understand the behaviour of the jobseekers in that particular market, and target with precision.

An old marketing adage states that, "50% of marketing works, we just don't know which 50%." The modern marketing professional will certainly not subscribe to this way of thinking, as marketing has become much more sophisticated over time. Where marketing is at its most sophisticated is in the use of data. Product marketing is driven by data and insight to ensure that the return on investment is maximised. The same must apply to recruitment marketing as well, and this targeted insight will not only be more cost-effective, but it is the route to finding the best people.

Using good data, you can identify how the best people in your target markets behave in a job market. Will they register with your job alert function? Do they wait for the approach on LinkedIn? Is it a market that a specialist agency dominates? Is there a trade press magazine or website that everybody reads? Is it a highly dynamic market which moves very quickly? Is it a market where there are many similar jobs advertised and candidates have an abundance of choice?

These considerations will inform how you speak to the candidates, what you say and how you deal with them in the process. This is your candidate segmentation—the lazy jobseekers, job board trawlers, social media candidates, etc. Better still speak to existing staff in different areas about what they do when they are looking. Do marketers look on marketingweek.com, did customer service staff all see the ad in local press, Facebook? Are there certain jobs that are only ever filled by agencies? Don't assume—use data and gather insight.

The trap to avoid is to develop the brand, use it tactically for advertisements at the point of need, and end up with unsatisfying results and unplanned agency dependency. Build the brand awareness and sentiment and with tactical deployment know what your target market will respond to and use the right channels. Make an informed choice about where you will access the candidates. Choose the channels you use, choices made on information you trust.

There has always been a traditional recruitment distinction between passive and active candidates. Those sitting happily with no idea about changing jobs and those who are *out there* job hunting. Technology and social media has blurred this popular distinction. The true passive candidate in the modern era is going to be hard to shift. They are locked in. However, most employees sit in that world between completely passive and actively looking. They are aware of the market. Remember how frequently people move around?

Brand building with messages that interest this population is powerful. It can also be a slow burner, but that might just indicate performance in current role. Passive, active and *aware*.

The channels for pushing the brand out and pushing opportunities for the roles as they emerge are as varied as they are for consumer branding. Online, press advertising, radio, bus shelter adverts, ad vans, leaflet drops, careers fairs, the job centre, television, social media, back of HGVs and so on. What do you have at your disposal? What product branding and marketing that your company does could be a part? Where can you use physical locations? Employee referral programmes? These are all opportunities to get that branding message to potential candidates to either create that feeling or notify them of an opportunity. Make informed decisions, that are part of a plan.

When it comes to the deployment of the brand the only limit is imagination. Auto Trader wanted to do something different and create a community for their contact centre recruitment in Manchester.

The advertising agency bought a van (from Auto Trader, of course) and dressed it up as a mobile disco and toured the streets of Manchester. The critical thing was, as Auto Trader is an online offering, the van advertised social media sites for people to go to.

Behind the fun and difference there was a sensible community-building concept, that was backed up by online activity as well. It was about profile raising and the event added an extra 500 followers to the company's recruitment social media site on Facebook.

What was also pleasing is that it changed perceptions. 41% of the visitors were females, which was up from the norm of 17%.

An effectively deployed branding message will drive candidates to your company website, so that once there they find jobs easily and are able to apply. The messaging on the website is the same as the branding. It's all seamless for the candidate.

APPLICATION CHANNELS

There are as many ways of advertising a specific role as there are of advertising a bar of soap. Your insight informs you of the candidate behaviour and that enables you to make informed choices as to which channel. Or which combination of channels. The goal is not to attract thousands of applications, the goal is to generate as many as you need to get the capability you want. Less is more.

The online job posting is the channel of choice for virtually every visible vacancy. For good reason. It's expected, it's easy and it's cheap. It's also often lazy, random and leaves the door open to a multitude of inappropriate applications. We saw earlier what most postings are like. Be different. Be selling. Be interesting and informative. Link to the brand.

Social media, and specifically, the business networking platform LinkedIn was proclaimed to revolutionise recruitment. With all this cheap and easy access, and an opportunity to engage directly with the candidate through in-platform communication channels this would surely herald the end of the world for all other forms of recruitment advertising communications. It's certainly a great tool, but things haven't quite panned out that way.

LinkedIn has certainly become a key candidate identification tool and it is used by a huge number of people to essentially advertise their careers and what they do. That is either with or without the desire to move jobs. It is easy for a recruiter to approach an individual about a specific role, unsolicited, and attain interest without all that messy advertising and application process. It has the potential candidate's work history right there in front of you. What could possibly go wrong?

For a start, it is a labour-intensive way of approaching people about a job. These are approaches to people who have, on the surface, expressed no indication of interest in your organisation whatsoever. They haven't responded to an advert, speculatively applied and for all you know they have no intention of moving.

The second time-consuming element is that social media is a communication channel, and once you open communication on a social media platform, you need to be prepared to invest time, resources and energy maintaining the dialogue. Potentially, dialogue with a lot of people, many of whom won't ever come to work for you.

There is no doubt that this is a fantastic tool, after all it is where most agency recruitment consultants find their candidates. Candidates they will place in a client at 20% of starting salary fees. (Clients who haven't adopted a strategic resourcing approach, of course.) Just be aware that it isn't the answer for everything and successful use requires knowledge and commitment. With available resource and as part of the strategic plan, it's a must-have for the toolkit.

The other social media channels are subtler in their interactions with recruitment. They are personal lives, the interaction of friends, sharing of experiences and expressing opinions. People aren't always at their most corporate or at their best on social media. But, it's a way of communicating with lots of people. However, the presence of corporate advertisements on social media can be seen as intrusive. The presence of recruitment advertising on Facebook in an effort to look like a cool place to work, can actually be counterproductive. It's a bit like dad dancing. Adverts on these sites are to be treated as with any potential advertising source, to be utilised if the insight indicates the value.

Social media is most definitely at its best for recruitment when utilised to build communities of candidates as part of an employer branding strategy. These communities must be developed around content, not just job advertisements. What is your business doing at the leading edge in their area of specialism? What articles can you publish that speak to certain markets? How can the discussion in these narrow communities enhance the brand that you have developed? Generating interesting content and building the community can be a potent addition to the branding strategy. Target specific markets, based on insight about what will excite the candidates you want to build a relationship with. Then, as the time comes to start recruiting, the community is already there.

The recruitment agency is not to be discounted, even as part of a strategic sourcing approach. That channel may be the best way of securing the best candidates for a specific market. For in-house recruitment teams, that is often complete anathema to the way they want to operate, and the pressure on recruitment cost will always steer the direction of travel away from the use of agencies where possible. The recruitment agency business thrives on the distress purchase, the perception of the buyer and lack of planning in organisations.

However, don't mistake this unplanned use of agencies as a sentiment that dismisses the whole industry as something that can be discarded with the right resourcing strategy. Recruitment agencies may well play a critical role in your sourcing mix. The reason is that you may well be looking to secure skills in very niche markets, where there are small numbers of suppliers who understand those niches extremely well. As a result, they know everybody in that sector, and subsequently everybody knows them and speaks to them when they want a move. They will also make direct approaches when they can sell your opportunity.

Yes, it would be more desirable for these candidates to come to you directly, for you to build the relationships and for the elimination of the broker. However, in a world of finite resources, that isn't always possible and it may ultimately be more expensive. It will certainly be time-consuming. You may never get the best people and in particularly tight markets, you certainly will not want to deny yourself what is possibly the most effective channel. The critical point is that you understand which markets these are and make the conscious choice that you will use the agency suppliers for those roles.

There are other practical aspects to this, that lie with the motivation of the recruitment firm. Firstly, knowing that they will be the sole supplier for that channel will secure their dedication, if there is any volume. Secondly, they can be managed to promote your brand in the market, as you would want it to be promoted. Thirdly, if you get them working right for you, you can ensure you are not wasting time and resource on the areas of recruitment that you trust the supplier with. You only have so much time and a problem solved frees up time and resource. Finally, if they are working for you, you can stop them from approaching your staff.

Dogmatic direct sourcing approaches where organisations aim to eliminate the use of recruitment agencies are laudable from a cost reduction viewpoint. Be careful though. Unless the employer branding message is so completely compelling as to reach everyone, there is always the risk that full agency eradication from the channel mix is short-term financial gain for the loss of access to important *passive/aware* candidate markets.

Make the use of agencies a conscious decision when it is what will work. Build mutually beneficial relationships with the agencies who can help where you need help.

That's the way with every channel. Developing the long-term capability plan creates the environment to understand the candidate behaviours and markets and act accordingly. Build the insight as to where the skills you want are, and use the tools to build communities and access the applications when needed.

If you have identified what you want the resourcing mix to be and the balance you want between hiring new talent, internal movement and developing talent, then you somehow need to be able to shift the dials on each channel. With external recruitment, you can ramp up or ramp down activity. But how do you turn up the internal market?

Firstly, generating supply from the internal market requires a culture that recognises its importance. There needs to be visibility of the available roles and a clear way to apply internally. However, visibility isn't enough.

As with all things that determine the health of an organisation in people matters the important thing is the attitude of line management. Line management firstly need to understand and endorse the reality of an internal market. They also need to recognise that it is a good thing for high-performing staff to want to move, but stay with the firm. If the move is in the interest of the individual and the interest of the firm they need to encourage the move and not even give a hint that such notions will be frowned upon. The idea of a line manager having to provide permission for someone to apply for internal jobs is patriarchal and impractical. You simply make it easier for them to move to competitors. That just doesn't make any sense.

If you really want to move the dial on internal mobility, that requires a greater degree of push. There are active measures that can be taken. Many organisations will hold internal careers fairs, where different departments demonstrate what is attractive about working there and what kinds of jobs they have. It's a great forum for people to explore opportunities, without putting themselves out there by way of applications. Storytelling brings the internal jobs market to life, it's all part of the branding for an internal market. Make sure that everyone knows how the internal market works, through directional advertising and give it a high profile.

Management culture is what really shifts the dial. Managers who not only accept that people will move on, but who actively encourage it within their team. Managers who will engage in career conversations with their staff, encompassing opportunities outside the immediate team. Having managers who will take a risk on an internal move with someone who doesn't quite have the right technical skills, but knows the organisation and has the right attitude. Managers who encourage their staff to move after two years in role.

If you really want to create a stir and an interesting debate, why not permit, or encourage internal headhunting? Any manager can make an approach to someone they like internally who would benefit their team. Give everyone profiles of talent across the business. That is at the radical edge, but doesn't it just put the individual at the heart of the process? It also probably happens anyway.

Management culture also defined how successful, or otherwise, talent management is. The *so what...?* of talent management for many people in the system is hugely damaging to the perception of what talent management is or does. Graduate programmes that have the graduate drift from department to department doing the photocopying erodes the importance of the need for entry-level talent. Or a graduate programme that can't really decide if it's there to build leaders or to develop technical specialists. These things are all fixable with the right direction and management input.

Firstly, your choice of what you are going to do with talent is linked to the strategic plan. You can then decide what you want to align its long-term objectives to. A lack of leadership in senior management? A shortage of skills in a critical area? An imperative to develop more in-house leaders? Build a graduate programme for future leaders? Whatever the driver is, again you will have made a conscious and informed decision to run with an approach to talent.

Keep it manageable, measurable, and something that managers and people on the talent programmes know what it is for, and what their role is. When everybody can understand the *why*, and it is easily articulated, it makes things much easier. *Catch-all* initiatives to record talent, when there simply isn't the headspace or opportunities is just storing trouble. The people that you have identified as high talent and want to nurture and keep are going to be interested in what that means for them. What that means for them is what role will they be doing in one year, two years, five years. It may not mean promotion, or money, or status. It may mean interest or stretch. But it comes down to opportunities. Not what training courses they will be going on. Not who their mentor will be, or the badge of being in a graduate or talent programme. They are signposts on the road, but the road must go somewhere.

That's the link to your strategic plan. Are there the opportunities for graduates to drop into? Is there the internal market for them to climb the ladder? Will your high-potential talent have the opportunities that meet their expectations? If you don't have the demand, don't create supply with a mismatched sense of expectation. If you have the strategic plan and the leadership sponsorship you won't need to. You adjust the dial accordingly.

Matching supply and demand for talent programmes forces the question. Is high-potential talent a shared resource to be moved around? How to get managers to release their high-performing staff? How to get managers to take a risk? Advertise the jobs openly, or keep for the few? Provide development and leave to the internal market? Have planned career paths? Tell the *talent* that they are *talent*?

There are no right and wrong answers. When you are making informed conscious decisions about how you want the resourcing mix to look and adjusting the mechanics to match, you give yourself the opportunity to think about why and how.

It's the same with temporary staff. Same with outsourcing. Eventually it will be the same with automation. Informed and conscious decision-making about where we want the supply to come from.

There is real power in a brand. Brands stir emotional, almost irrational reactions. There are employer brands that people are drawn too without any real knowledge of the pay and conditions, working environment or prospects (Google? Rolls Royce? Facebook?). Likewise, there are brands that people are repelled from.

Most organisations sit in the middle. However, the brand is no less important, because it already exists. People will have a view, or create a view when they start interacting with the business. Understand it, understand what the message to promote is and choose the right channels to do so.

Generating enough candidates for jobs that are of sufficient quality is founded in insight. Insight about candidates and insight about how to access them. A strategic and long-term capability plan illustrates which markets to build the insight for.

The focus on quality takes time and investment and trust in the plan. That applies equally to the growth of internal capability. Nurturing a vibrant jobs market, or ensuring that talent has a career path to grow into.

Make informed decisions.

CHAPTER II
SCREENING AND SELECTION

"Marry in haste, repent at leisure."

William Congreve

Planning and preparation are the keys that unlock recruitment markets. They are also the cornerstones of success when deciding who is best for a role. Plan assessment of candidates thoroughly and thoughtfully.

You need to understand what success looks like in the role. What are the characteristics, traits and skills that will enable the individual to excel? What do you need to discover about the individual that will enable them to thrive in the organisation? What are the attributes that will help them be successful?

What you are looking for is a great employee, as opposed to a great candidate. A great candidate is someone who does well in the assessment scenario, and a great employee is someone who does well in the job. The two things are not always a direct correlation. How do you narrow the gap between identifying a great candidate and them emerging as a great employee?

That shouldn't be difficult. However, assessing fit for the roles in the plan is a significant challenge if not done correctly. Having the right assessment depends on more than just understanding the job and person specifications. You will also need to understand the limitations of the assessment tools you are using, and even more critically the capability of the people using them. The best planning and best tools are rendered useless in the wrong hands. That's an issue that is a constant challenge.

What we want to always do is increase the probability of having the right resource in place at the right time to deliver against our plan. Assessing to get the right person in that role is the part of that exercise that is hugely impactful, positively or negatively.

What makes it so difficult? Quite simply a recruitment decision is a complex decision. (Literally. A common psychology definition describes a complex decision as a situation, "where there are many alternatives and/or where attributes of alternatives are difficult to understand".) More than that it's a complex decision that involves a person at both ends in a sort of dance/first date/game.

Both participants (individual and the organisation) are making a decision. Does this person have the technical skills? Can they lead? How are they under pressure? Will they fit with the team?

At the same time... Can I work for this guy? What is the culture like? Will I like my team? What are the politics?

By the time you get to assessment all the hard, identifiable facts *should* be clear for each protagonist. What the last job was, what the pay is, etc. But the nitty-gritty stuff is a moving target.

It is rare that either side will be one hundred percent honest in the interview process. That adds to the complexity somewhat. So, at the same time as trying to identify if the words uttered by the other side of the table are appealing, both sides also must decide if they are true.

If that makes selection sound like it's a confrontational environment of mistrust and subterfuge, it's because so often it is. Trick questions, snap judgements, bias and practice that assesses nothing relevant abound. Interviewing is the land of the amateur expert and it is heavily populated with people who believe they are great judges of talent or of other people. The self-congratulation behind the hire that is a star becomes amnesia about the failures. The truth is that much is random. The blind squirrel looking for an acorn.

It appears like cycling uphill against the wind when it comes to making the right decision. The candidates are embellishing their achievements. The interviewers rarely hire, or are buoyed with their own brilliance, or blinded by bias, or average at interviewing, or at times actually very good. Truth is, interviewing capability is universally inconsistent.

In addition, the pressure is always on, and whoever is hiring *needs* to get the job filled. Time with the position vacant is time lost. That encourages judgemental generosity. Somehow through this you need to get the right decisions made as frequently as possible.

The secret is that there is no secret. You are more likely to be successful if there is a thought-through plan and it's executed with care and precision. You aim to remove the pressure points from the process and compensate for weaknesses. Getting quality is not just about being good at interviewing, not by a long shot.

Consider the point of the branding activity and building communities. The reason for doing this is not simply to take pressure off the numbers that you will require, but also to get quality applicants in at the front end of the process. Quality in at the front end improves your chances as you move through the process. The key is to pick that out from the rest. The space to build these communities is created by the strategic workforce plan, and the branding communication that goes along with it. That is where the strategic plan starts to have its impact on the eventual quality of what you are hiring according to your requirements.

The principle for tactical candidate generation is the same. The assessment of who will end up in the role starts at this point and it starts with the candidate. When you come to the tactical deployment of advertising you need to ensure that you impress those you want and you put off those you do not. A great advertisement is as likely to make the unsuitable candidate back away as make the good candidate apply. Generating the right candidates, through effective branding and candidate generation, is where the path to the quality of hiring begins.

When it comes to assessment, it is useful to think about this in two distinct parts. There is screening and then there is selection. Screening is a function of exclusion and selection is picking the best. Much of the focus from psychologists and academia is naturally on the selection part, how to interview, best practice in testing, etc. However, effective screening can really do the heavy lifting.

The principle is simple. If you are generating high-quality applications from both outside and inside the organisation, and you can narrow that longlist of candidates to a shortlist of candidates where even the worst choice is a good choice, then the reality is the quality of the interview that takes place is less likely to do damage. If we are in a scenario where there is a part of the process (say the interview) where we cannot control the quality of that activity, then assume the worst and minimise its impact. Improving the capability of the organisation is about improving the probability of getting it right in each individual selection. Therefore, investing more time and effort in attraction and screening rather than complexity in assessment makes sense.

This isn't saying that there are vast swathes of interviewing incompetence in every business. What we do know by pretty much every judge of reliability and validity in assessment decisions is that an interview is an unreliable tool, even in the best hands. The interview is the preferred tool of assessment and, as stated above, it is subject to bias, and suffers in terms of predictive validity.

The baseline academic work in defining predictive validity in recruitment assessment is *The Validity and Utility of Selection Methods in Personnel Psychology: Practical and Theoretical Implications of 85 Years of Research Findings* by Schmidt and Hunter in 1998. (Catchy title, bit of a holiday read.) On a ranking of predictive validity where zero is random person from the street and one is the right person for the job, unstructured interviewing gets a score of 0.3 and skilled, structured interviewing a score of 0.6. Note, the key word in that sentence is skilled. There have been developments in assessment and other studies done, but most scoring settles on figures close to this. The fundamental point is that by itself even a structured interview in skilled hands isn't brilliant.

So, even in the right hands and well-constructed, the interview is a bit hit-and-miss. However, the structured interview is much favoured in most advanced organisations to improve the reliability and validity. The competency-based interview (CBI) is the assessment tool of choice in most large businesses, and for good reasons. However, the very first thing a CBI will identify is who is good at preparing for a CBI. Better than an unstructured interview? Definitely. High probability of guaranteed success? Not so much.

Undertaking a CBI that really gets to the heart of a matter and identifies the truths about performance takes a skilled practitioner. Undertaking a structured interview that puts the candidate at ease is also no easy thing. It's not a casual twice a year guarantees expertise type of thing.

Then there is bias. We all have it, no matter what we think. Most often it isn't one of the headline-grabbing biases. It may not even be a prejudice that you know you have, or remotely exhibit. However, we all will make a judgement on someone that is not directly future role performance related, but assumes from our own view of the world. It's as likely to be a positive bias as it is a negative bias. Ginger-haired people are smarter. Fat people are lazy. Blue eyes mean stupidity. Tall people are good leaders. Women are hysterical. Men are feckless. There are multiple academic studies to illustrate that attractive people are far more likely to do well in interviews than unattractive people. Bias is a significant factor.

There is a strange paradox in the application of assessment structure. Ironically, as the decision becomes more complex the tools used to make the decisions often become less so. Many organisations will have an industrial process for assessing their entry-level staff. Not a bad thing, they talk to the customers after all. Important to identify the right criteria for the front line.

The process is less *scientific* and more gut-feel and personal-judgement based as you move up the corporate scale. The complexity at senior management level in terms of fit (politics, leadership, personal circumstances, team fit, strategic capability, etc.) is much more complex than at customer service level (transactional problem-solving, empathy, etc.) and the cost of failure is much more significant.

So, a major investment decision for an organisation, with potentially damaging consequences, is made by unskilled people with ineffective tools and a high chance of a decision resting on something that isn't role related.

There are three ways to get to grips with this issue. Ensure that the candidate generation and screening before interview is so effective that even the worst selection decision at interview can't be a bad decision. Change the tools at selection to make sure that they have a higher degree of reliability and validity. Improve the skills of the people doing the interviewing. Better still, do a combination of all three.

EVALUATING WHAT TO ASSESS

Planning and preparation is the next not-so-secret, secret. Start with a thorough evaluation of the role that you need to fill. As well as using the data to inform the content of your advertising, agency briefing, social media searching, it will also define the characteristics that you want to assess against. It sounds simple, but so often this is rushed, or taken from an old role profile, or what the person vacating the job was like. The key is to understand what success will look like in the role. What are the tasks that the job holder needs to do to be successful? What skills do they need? What qualifications do they need? What are the characteristics that they will need to demonstrate? What does good look like? Are there examples of successful job holders that can be used as a template for skills and behaviours?

This all needs to be established before the work to fill the role begins. The information gathered at the outset not only informs the assessment approach, but defines the insight as to how the candidates might be identified. Are they likely to already be in the business, what salary level is the job, and what is the best way of reaching them? Planning and preparation may be a fundamental element of the strategy of resourcing, but when it comes down to each role or campaign it is just as important at a tactical level.

Good assessment design is building something that predicts job performance. The assessment process should gather evidence to predict how the subject of the assessment will perform in the role. Good performance or bad performance in interview should reflect good or bad performance in the role. Assessment 1.1. However, there are traps to avoid. Assumptions about what good performance is, as opposed to observation of *actual* good performance. The criteria need to be observable and measurable in a consistent and fair manner. More traps, particularly when a hiring manager expresses the desire for certain personality traits. A focus on technical skills is a further trap—frequently fallen into with the professions, where the behaviours that lead to role success are overlooked in favour of qualifications. Not only do you need to design an assessment process that reflects the criteria for success in the role, but you must also weight that evidence in favour of the key, or critical elements of performance.

The biggest mistake committed in selection preparation is to not do it for the sake of saving time, or where there isn't a perception of value in putting in the upfront effort. When there are many of the same role recruited, and the jobs are simple, the job analysis and subsequent assessment path should be a straightforward implementation. However, you may recall Company A from Chapter five where they singularly failed to recognise the sales element. Or Company B where they wanted social media expertise. Or Insurance Company C who valued teamwork. It requires a clarity of focus and a real determination to unpick what the successful factors for success in the role are, and not what they are perceived to be.

Where few value such rigour in design, is often when there is recruitment of individual jobs, IT roles, accountants, risk managers, marketing executives, HR positions, etc. By not going through the same, thorough process of job analysis and assessment design, aligned to the criteria for future success, there is often an assumption that the CV sift and interview will do the trick. The evidence suggests otherwise.

SCREENING

The criteria you pick out here can be used in various ways across advertising, screening and selection to streamline. When it comes to using them in advertising the principle is straightforward. What are the characteristics the job holder must have that will encourage candidate self-deselection? The must-haves that you have identified that can be highlighted to the candidates that they progress no further without these. These will not be personal traits. They will not be competencies. People will not exclude themselves from applying based on *Role holder must have excellent teamworking and communication skills*, or *Outgoing personality required*.

It's more tangible things that work. Shift times, professional qualifications required, technical skills needed, etc. These are the effective filters. You have built a community with the branding and getting the right ones from those is the next stage of whittling to the perfect candidate. There are simple things too—make sure the job title is not confusing jargon or ambiguous. It needs to speak to the candidates who want to do that job. They need to understand what it is from that first glance.

Assuming the community is strong and the advertising specific, screening is the chance to get that longlist down to a shortlist, all of whom ideally can do the job. So, what is the right number for a shortlist? There isn't a right number. There are some wrong numbers though. *One* is not a great answer—rightly or wrongly, a hiring manager will always want to make a comparison. *Can I see one more?* is poor. A manageable number, but all of quality. Right skills, availability, salary level, qualifications, and even behaviours, attitude. (Advertising salaries is something some organisations like and some don't. There isn't a right answer. What is most definitely a wrong answer is to get to interview stage with a mismatch. Brand damaging and time-consuming.)

The classic and old-fashioned way of screening who goes forward is the CV scan. Piles of CV for *yes/no* and *maybe*. Remember, a CV is a self-certified document and although massive fabrications are rare there is an inevitable amount of embellishment. They serve a purpose for sure, but there are many tools that can make the screening process a genuine quality refinement in a way a CV sift cannot.

There are numerous tools that can be used—*killer* questions, online situation judgement tests, ability tests, technical tests, telephone interview or video interviews. Most applicant tracking systems will have the capability to either construct testing in the system or integrate with test suppliers. Carefully contrived series of screening tests based on the role essentials are the best way of constructing a high-quality shortlist, that reduces the impact of human bias and gives you the best chance of candidates at the selection stage that could all do the job effectively. Then it's down to choosing which is the best.

The key with careful screening is that they relate to the job success criteria that you have established. It's about the quality of the tool being used. For example, situational judgement tests have been around for over 75 years in selection exercises (but not always called situational judgement tests) and give the candidate hypothetical scenarios, asking them to come up with an answer. Where they are particularly applicable in screening is that they can be designed to be absolutely job specific, put online in multiple choice, accurately scored, clearly linked to the job in the candidate's mind and the scores can be ranked. However, they need to be skilfully assembled, to avoid candidates giving right answers by simple common sense as opposed to job knowledge.

Technical testing is easy to apply when it fits. Jobs where a high degree of technical knowledge is critical. IT roles are the typical examples. If applied well in screening, it can leave the selection part of the interview to deal with the *softer* elements of what success looks like. Avoid the trap of technical testing followed by an entirely technical interview.

The telephone interview is a great way to screen candidates, if implemented correctly. There are two general forms of telephone interview. Firstly, the *volume* telephone interview, used to process high numbers of applicants for lower level jobs. Structured, scored, repetitive. It is also commonly used as a follow-up to a CV screen at managerial, technical level. A conversation to understand if the basic requirements are met, if there is an appetite to proceed on both sides and usually more free-flowing than the structured approach for volume hiring.

It's great, but telephone interviewing can be very labour intensive. Particularly if the volume of applications exceeds expectation or desire. It is a logistical exercise to arrange, again a draw on time and resource. As it is a conversation, it is also a two-way street, the candidate will also have questions.

They are most effective when the telephone interview has a purpose, and is designed to establish specific screening criteria. Replicable screening criteria. Short, structured, scored telephone interviews for volume applicants can be a blunt, but very effective way to bring candidate numbers to a manageable size. At managerial level, the telephone interview can delve behind the CV to understand if the depth of experience is as required, or what the motivation is.

The traps to avoid is the telephone conversation becoming a full interview. Or the questions on the telephone being repeated at interview. Or the telephone interview being a general *chat*, with no real screening purpose.

A telephone interview can enhance the candidate experience, as it is also a chance for the candidate to screen. They can take the opportunity to ask questions and make their decision about progressing. It can also be an awful candidate experience if the candidate isn't expecting the call, or doesn't know that the call is an interview, or is made to feel uncomfortable because the structure is too rigid. All avoidable.

Video interviewing is a growing area. Particularly with what is defined as *asynchronous video interviewing*. A technical way of saying the candidate records their answer, which is stored and viewed later. The intention is to remove the logistical challenge of arranging the telephone interview.

CERN, the European laboratory for particle physics, is one of the world's largest and most respected centres for scientific research. They invited the video interviewing company SONRU in to help them streamline recruitment. It was expensive and logistically difficult to accommodate candidates from all over Europe and their feel was that video interviewing would ease that burden.

They were also pleased with a surprise benefit. By being able to see and hear the candidates, rather than just read a CV, they could get so much more about the individual and make better choices. Yes, that certainly saved time, but (being scientists) when they ran the video interview process against the former process as a test, they saw an appreciable increase in quality of candidate at interview. That is the very essence of making the face-to-face interview difficult to get wrong.

Many organisations love a psychometric personality test in their recruitment, but there are sensible reasons not to include them. It's worth saying of course, that personality and work preferences are without doubt important for success in any role. The first issue is that for the test to be successful there must be empirical data to support the validity of the outcome of the test and how that relates to job performance. Basically, we may think that the role requires a certain personality type, but if we are going to use data to measure the type, we need data to compare it to.

The next issue is that, despite what the designers of such tests will tell you, they can be played, they are largely known entities, and in a selection scenario some candidates will almost certainly pick the answers they think you are looking for. The final reason is that when used as part of a selection process they become disproportionate when weighing the evidence. In any assessment where there are different pieces of evidence it is a common trait of human nature to trust what is seen as the *science* in what is a complex decision. It is the one thing that will appear to the untrained eye as the irrefutable truth, and will determine the decision over all other evidence.

It should be said that as a development tool, psychometrics most certainly have a valuable place. They are great, interesting, motivational and insightful. Not so great for selection.

The branding has created a great community. The data driven attraction methods have generated high calibre applications. The internal market has augmented this with some great people. They have been screened with modern and accurate tools to give us a shortlist. The shortlist is of exceptional quality, and very enthused. Everything is going to plan.

SELECTION

Next up is the selection stage, or most commonly, the interview. Of course, because the attraction and screening has been so excellent all you need to do is give the manager a tombola and put in the names of the remaining candidates. No bad decision possible, so let's save time and get that tombola fired up.

Despite the ease of implementation, reasonable success chances and fun potential, the tombola approach is not in the strategic resourcing handbook. Hiring managers would hate it (or would they?) and it's most definitely a poor candidate experience. Forget that one.

Regardless of how good the screening is, to ensure that you really give yourself the best chance of making the best capability choice, you need to make a selection decision. Despite the reliability and validity concerns about the tool, an interview will be a part of that selection process. Why, given its lack of reliability?

The two people in the process will both want it. It's a human connection. The hiring manager will never really accept any decision that they haven't had the *whites-of-their-eyes* experience. It's an integral part of the process for the candidate to make their judgement too. Make it as effective as possible and back up the evidence gathered in that meeting with all the other evidence.

A retail business, Company A, had a process where HR conducted the entire hiring process, including interviews as they didn't trust the competence of store managers.

Turnover was the issue when the managers did the recruitment. The high turnover problem was attributed to poor hiring decisions and the solution was to hand things over to HR. This made a lot of people happy. The managers didn't have to bother with this pesky recruitment lark, and the recruitment team felt a sense of complete ownership of an important process. It was an expensive solution, however, as the recruitment team became a vast army of interviewers. But, the saving in staff turnover would surely pay for the extra HR staff?

The solution didn't quite work as intended. Short-term turnover of people leaving within the first three months of joining dropped as a direct result of the change. Completely inappropriate hiring was eliminated, with the HR team doing an effective screening job. Overall turnover, however, barely shifted at all.

The managers didn't feel they *owned* the new joiner as they showed up for duty on the first day. The new joiner also felt no connection with their new boss. Right from the start there was a lack of investment on both sides. Then, when things didn't work out, the manager always had HR to blame. Which happened a lot, because the overall level of managerial capability was low.

Those promoted to management positions were the top sales performers. Rarely a direct correlation with management aptitude. Staff weren't leaving before because of bad recruitment, they were leaving because of bad management. That problem was untouched. Therefore, staff satisfaction and turnover stayed the same.

The best approach is an assessment centre. Multiple sources of evidence for multiple traits, viewed by multiple assessors. All based on the success criteria and all the assessors well trained in the assessment methodologies and knowledgeable of the criteria and the job. These are commonplace for graduate recruitment, contact centre recruitment, and other volume roles. Multiple assessment exercises in sequence with measurable outcomes, discussed by a number of assessors. There is no right or wrong for the number of assessment exercises, or the number of stages. It's a balance between gathering all the evidence you need against the experience of the candidate and their willingness to keep turning up.

Of course, an assessment centre isn't always practical for a number of reasons, but the underlying principle is not to be avoided. Making the best choice will be more likely if more evidence (of likely success at the role) is gathered, and if there are secondary pieces of evidence for the key criteria that back up what is covered in the interview. Workplace sample tests for example—exercises that reflect what the job will entail.

An interview will continue to be a core element of selection, so the key is to make sure that the interview time is used as efficiently as possible. There will be a finite period with each candidate, so that is the opportunity for both parties to get from it what they need by way of evidence of a match. The time in that interview is precious for the interviewer to extract the evidence that is needed. Evidence predicting future job performance, not evidence about hobbies, or football teams, or the commute, or anything else that isn't directly specific to the job. What those things might tell an interviewer is that they like the person, or the person is like them and therefore likely to fit in well. The interviewer might decide that is important to success. However, unless it is identified as one of the assessment success criteria for the role, it is irrelevant.

It's important to put the candidate at ease and that, in itself, is a skill. Any candidate is much more likely to talk freely when they are at ease in an interview situation. That talking freely then helps the interviewer gather evidence. The evidence is to support the notion that they are hitting what is needed or not. A structured interview is much better than an unstructured interview, and there are good solid reasons for that distinction.

An unstructured meandering through experience may reveal a great many things, but in a structured interview you can make sure the things that are revealed are pertinent. The structure of the interview will be about the role characteristics. Remember, time is precious. A well-managed, structured interview can keep the candidate on-track and guide them towards putting their best foot forward. A structured interview will provide a common baseline for all candidates, enabling comparison.

The most common type of structured interview is the CBI, and in the right hands this can be an effective method of identifying what the candidate has really contributed in their career. Understanding what they have done, is a good indicator of what they are likely to do. Organisations like them—they fit with a competency framework, and it keeps things neatly tied up. They can be scored and defended if someone cries, "Foul!". They are easy to understand and with pre-defined interview questions about the same competency, they are easy to conduct. Easy to conduct to a *level*. It's a compromise where the calibre of interviewer is variable. Better to have a poorly executed good tool, than no rigour at all.

In the right hands. A skilled interviewer with a CBI can make it feel like a natural conversation, whilst probing for evidence (positive and negative) and linking that to job performance. If someone is lying, the skilled interviewer will catch them out. If someone has a great story but isn't articulating it well, the interviewer can draw it out from them, and understand that not being great in an interview doesn't mean not being great in the job. With attraction, screening and supporting selection exercises, a CBI conducted with skill is a further good producer of evidence.

However, many organisations that have them as their core selection tool, put them in the hands of less skilled interviewers and then they can have the same reliability as an unstructured interview. Although, critically they are more defendable, of course. Many candidates will have taken CBIs and many know how to answer the questions, the best candidates (not necessarily the best employees, of course) will adopt the STAR technique and frame their answer in *situation, task, action* and *result*. The unknowing candidate may not do this naturally and the unskilled interviewer may not seek it.

As roles become more senior the competencies or skills required to make things happen in an organisation are not neatly compartmentalised in a single competency answer. An example a senior manager will give to respond to one competency question (the old, "Tell me about a time when...") will cover a range of skills and attributes. An unskilled interviewer following the instruction on the interview pack, may ignore all the other good evidence for other competences. Furthermore, a knowing candidate with a poor interviewer can wax lyrical about a project they led and how they made it all happen, when perhaps they were a team member and not the leader. It requires skill in interviewing to get under the bonnet of the candidate's stories.

Another watch-out for the CBI is the tendency for them to favour the internal candidate. If you have opportunities open to internal and external candidates at the same time, the organisation's CBI is likely to favour the internal candidate. Quite simply they will be familiar with the language the interview uses, and often they will have seen the actual questions. Be careful with organisational references in the interview questions of a CBI to avoid them being jargonised for the internal audience.

The reality is, however, that an interview is something the hiring manager will expect to do. Make it as robust and helpful, candidate friendly and reliable as possible. Structure in the interview provides this better than any other form, and there are other ways to structure than just a CBI. A structured interview, with a scoring methodology conducted by two people with rigorous note taking.

Executive selection has the most significant negative impact if done incorrectly. The decisions to appoint are made by more senior individuals, and whereas these may be immensely talented individuals, that doesn't mean to say they are also the most gifted at making hiring judgements on the ability of someone else to do a job. What it does mean, is that they are the most likely to believe that that have supreme ability to make these judgements.

Executive selection can often be based on the most baseless of things. For example, "If they did the job at ABC PLC, they must be good. They always have good people.". Informal references are commonplace, "Good guy/not a good guy/didn't work out". These are, of course, almost entirely subjective, but are often taken as gospel. Interviews are often no more than chats.

There are numerous peer interviews (also chats), where the view given is as much a political view as an objective assessment view. Many organisations now put in a check to what can be these subjective measures in the form of an interview with an occupational psychologist, exploring motivation, ways of thinking, experience, etc. An improvement, but most executives will have experienced such sessions, know what their profile is and realise they can work it in their favour without ever being misleading.

At senior level, the principles of good assessment do not change. The decision-making is more complex and the criteria sit at a different level of complexity, but that does not undermine the fundamental basis of what you are attempting to do. Understand the key success criteria of the role and identify those characteristics in the candidates. The trouble is that at senior level there is a belief that senior candidates would not undertake a range of assessments. After all, they have a track record. It just isn't a track record for the job in question in the organisation in question.

Virgin Money choose the route of an assessment centre for their recruitment of a new and critical executive role, when they created an *immersive assessment event*. They were looking for someone to lead innovation to "Uncover innovative products and services to help make money friendly again." So, they developed "The most creative job interview ever," to assess for leadership and innovation.

In a constructed event, the candidates moved through a series of rooms, each with a different challenge, reflecting aspects of the role, in a playful way. A football team requiring a half-time pep-talk to test leadership. Another tested their skills of improvisation by asking them to write the lyrics to a song about to be recorded by a piano-playing lounge singer. They were met by an actor in a smoke-filled room telling them they "Have just three minutes to suggest as many possible places they could be right now." This looked at creativity and fluency in quickly generating lots of fresh ideas.

Is this an example of textbook assessment? No—but it tied elements of the role to exercises and had ways of measuring that. Importantly, the candidates were more than willing to engage in the process. They loved it, in fact. The agency who designed it also used it as a PR tool, and it spoke perfectly to the right audience.

The result was they had ten executive-level candidates willing to go through this and they recruited precisely what they wanted. The successful candidate was an innovator from outside the financial services industry, the guy who created Shazam. It was creative, off-the-wall and not for everyone, but it shows that executive assessment needn't be so staid. This illustrates that, even at senior level, the approaches of branding and thoughtfulness at assessment are the approaches which work.

INTERVIEWER CAPABILITY

The final thing you can do is improve the quality of the interviewers. Typically, this is a problem solved with the introduction of a sheep dip, one-day interview skills training programme, that will have little lasting impact for those who do not interview regularly. There are however, innovative ways to address the issue.

Aspirant is a company that address the inconsistencies of interviewing quality issues using data. Their sweet spot currently exists with large professional services, where recruitment is for many of the same role. The interviewers should all be looking for the same thing.

They took a large professional services firm (10,000+) and defined what a successful hire was. This was based on performance and tenure of over two years. So, in the role, doing well and sticking around. They created a matrix of how the interviewing manager performed—what their decision was, how did that match against the other interviewer and what the outcome was. Sounds complex, but in essence it was a "Did they get it right?" question. The *positive* outcome for a decline was that the candidate didn't last two years somewhere else. Aspirant tracked all the declined candidates to build the data set.

The output from the analysis was revealing. The average success rate of the interviewers was 47%, which is moderately worse than a coin toss. They also discovered that a small number of the interviewers, some six from a total of 44 had a very high success rate. The *so-what* of this story is they could identify the success characteristics of the *good* interviewers and introduce them to the not-so-gifted.

What is alarming from the Aspirant analysis of managerial interviewing standards is that they conducted their analysis in an environment that should foster consistency and interviewing success. Each hiring manager was a senior manager and they were all technical experts, hiring junior practitioners. If these managers are only getting it right half of the time, then how are managers in more complex hiring environments faring?

This is difficult. There will be hiring managers who recruit frequently. Clearly, it is critical that they are skilled and understand the tools of assessment and value rigour. There will also be managers who recruit infrequently, but appoint significant roles. They also need to be skilled.

Sheep dip is of limited use and having a skilled third-party interviewer take over is a poor candidate experience, poor managerial experience and resource heavy. The best approach is to understand the interviewing population, frequency, importance of hire and capability. This is a major consideration when it comes to operating model. The quality of assessor can have a massive impact on the whole system. The decision of how to manage will be one of informed choices, and choosing which compromise is the most palatable. What is the capability? How often do the hire? What level of support is required? What level of support is realistic?

The problem is eased somewhat, if attraction and screening has taken care of that heavy lifting.

THE CANDIDATE

Do not forget the candidate experience through the assessment process. Doing the right thing to assess for the role should enhance the candidate experience. Firstly, a thought-through assessment that is defined in advance will be something you can tell the candidate about. Communication is key and they want to know what is happening.

A good candidate experience does not mean an *easy* candidate experience in assessment. A good candidate experience leaves the applicant safe in the knowledge that they have been rigorously assessed against the requirements of the role. Success means something and failure is easy to understand. Not emerging from an interviewing saying, "What on earth was that about?" Not taking a psychometric test where they guess what you are looking for. It should make sense, be obviously linked to the role and transparent. And be understanding of the needs of the candidate.

If the job is a part-time evening job, the applicant has probably applied because that fits their lifestyle. Interview in the evening. Where possible, give the candidate choices for when they are interviewed. Where the options are limited give them plenty of notice. Don't make them feel expendable by shifting things about. Respect their time, by not having long waits and pointless gaps and meaningless chats.

The assessment process is one where a change in execution excellence can have a dramatic impact in uplifting organisational capability over time. It sits at the heart of the process, and requires attention and thoughtfulness. It is also complicated and it is easy to understand why the decision is a difficult one, why so many rely on gut instinct and why ultimately so many recruitment assessment decisions don't work out as planned.

Most organisations of any scale, whether they recognise it or not, will have variable performance from the people doing the interviewing. This is impacting the candidates, impacting the calibre of hire and ultimately impacting the brand. The key is to make bad decisions as difficult as possible. Prepare thoroughly, use the brand and advertising that attracts the people you want to attract and deters the people you want deterred. Screen, based on the criteria that demonstrate success in role, use more than just an interview and help interviewers become better at the task.

Assessment success is wrapped up in the essential conditions for strategic resourcing success. The business leadership needs to understand that this is not a task of insignificance that can be entrusted to the unskilled but confident. They need to recognise the importance of getting it right, and the impact good or bad assessment has on capability.

The strategic workforce plan long-term view will provide the information to design assessment for those key skills. What you look for in great staff becomes a conscious decision.

Investment in screening tools saves many hours of management time at assessment centre, or interview. Yes, there is complexity in justifying the spend over here for time saved over there, but the goal is improving capability. Saving time and money is the icing on the cake. As for the manager who wants to recruit and is hard-pressed for time to put in the preparation to build attraction or do the job analysis for the assessment, they will surely appreciate the time saved in having to manage fewer underperformers or starting all over again.

With planning and thinking, you can make it difficult to make a bad decision, and likely to make many more excellent ones.

Hire Power

CHAPTER 12
THE CANDIDATE

"The difference between something good and something great is attention to detail."

Charles R. Swindoll

In any process that involves resourcing, be that a talent process, a recruitment process or internal mobility there are ultimately just two people involved. Someone who needs to hire to hit their objectives and someone who will move into that vacant role. With scale, it is easy to fall into thinking in terms of an industrial process and focus on the big numbers, however success lies with two individuals getting what they need, repeated many times.

The role the manager with the gap in her team will play in any resourcing activity will depend on the operating model of HR that surrounds her. In some organisations that will involve them doing a great deal more than in others, and that will often be a design forced by convenience and budget.

As we have seen in earlier chapters, if that activity encompasses brand building, candidate generation and assessment design the road to capability improvement will be not just difficult, but blocked. However, in all operating model design, the devil is in the detail and the hiring manager will always feel more comfortable with some control, engagement and oversight of their hiring.

Truth is, the detail is critical in a process involving the movement of people. Who tells the candidate when to show up? Who books the room? Who re-books the room after a cancellation? Who prints off the CV before an interview? Who attends the interview? Who records the interview? Who makes the offer? And so on. The individual here is the hiring manager and it is essential that from the outset they know what their role is. Who does what and when. How the process works.

Managers generally dislike the administrative parts of a process, and in moving people around there are always many administrative activities. If there is leadership and management understanding that this is a critical activity, then sharing this burden is easier. Where there is a view that resourcing does administrative things only, then that is a different challenge. Whatever the balance is in the operating model the necessity is that everybody knows and understands their role and the importance of each of the moving parts.

For the external candidate, the internal applicant or the high talent individual being appointed into a senior role, the very first thing we need to be aware of is that this is a moment in their lives that has much more importance to them than it does to us. This is the dream job, the first job, the big move, the pay rise that gets the holiday they wanted, freedom from a nightmare boss, the company they have always wanted to work for, the job to get them through university. More often than not, they'll discuss it with friends and family, project the possibilities in life and agonise over the decision. Whatever it is for them, it means more than filling a vacancy.

Companies tend to view a candidate experience as something that is beneficial to their process. It is often an add-on, or an afterthought. A project, even: *Enhancing the candidate experience*. It deserves a little more focus that that. Without the slightest hint of hyperbole, resourcing is a function of HR that changes people's lives. When you are changing someone's life, it is not to be taken lightly.

That individual in the process is deserving of some basics of treatment throughout. Honesty, transparency, communication, fairness. It's often just a matter of you thinking how you would want to be treated, and doing the same. There is an obvious and huge benefit to the organisation of this approach too. Any candidate experience survey tells the same story. Treat a candidate well, they stay. Don't, and they might drop out.

The experience starts before application. The individual employee or potential applicant has to see something in you, as an employer, that they want. The brand that appeals to them. That branding, or the *tone of voice* of the branding should also be consistent through the process. Of course, the external branding work will be the positive (but honest) aspects of the organisation, but as the process continues and the candidate gets deeper into it, you need to also understand how they feel about and will adapt to the downsides. For staff, they need to recognise the employer brand as something they feel a part of, that it is reflective of their working experience. These things can only be achieved through quality EVP development.

There will still be an advertisement, a direct approach, or a conversation with an agency that launches the individual application for the role. We have seen examples of online advertisements that are full of words, jargon and pointless detail for that part of the process. What the person who is interested in the brand needs to decide before they become a candidate for a specific role, is whether they are right for the role and the role is right for them. At this point that individual is making the decision. If the branding is marketing, that initial role contact is a sales pitch. Of course, good sales is not about deception, but about matching needs.

The job title is important. You may call your marketing manager the "Boss Weaver of Customer Dreams" but your candidate certainly doesn't. People first become candidates when they see a job title that they recognise as one they are doing or that they aspire to. From that point, the candidate will want more and more information, some of which is dependent on level, some of which isn't. Simple facts at the start of the process and more information as it continues.

Where is the job based? What is the reward for the job? What are the main responsibilities? Who is the boss? What is the company like? What skills do I need to apply? What qualifications? What experience? Will this job fulfil my ambitions? How do I apply? What's the process? When do I need to apply by? When is the expected start?

The message about the job should be clear, regardless of whether it's spoken by an in-house researcher, a recruitment consultant or in an advertisement. More information can be sent separately, made available on a website, or discussed later in the process. Clarity in essential information, attractive, allied to brand, gives compelling reasons for the qualified to apply, with a clear call to action.

Through assessment, it's about clear communication—what, why and when. Times that suit. Candidate choice where possible. Information about the people interviewing them. In the interview, there should be no tricks and a clear explanation of what is going to happen. Tests and other assessments should be clear in their objective and the purpose obvious to the candidate. A good candidate experience is by no means a compromise on rigour—it doesn't have to be an easy assessment—just fair and relevant.

Communication is the number one thing that candidates value through the process. Knowing what is happening and when. Bear in mind the emotions the candidate will be feeling. They have hope and expectation on application, and if that application is allowed to sit without a response, with no recognition of the effort in showing interest in your organisation, you are missing an opportunity to make a great impression. Rejection will be disappointing, but can be managed with clear justification. This is tough when there are thousands of applications, but it shouldn't be ignored. Technology can help.

As the candidates progress to interview the excitement and anticipation will increase. They will undertake research, put in more effort. Book time off work. Cancelling the interview late in the day may be an easy cancellation for the manager if there is a meeting that comes up, but is a let-down to the candidate. The candidate may not have done research or booked the time off work, or got a babysitter, or bought a new suit, but they may have and to so wilfully disregard the effort they've put in sends a very loud message about how the organisation and that manager in particular treat people. Cancellations happen, but they should really be a last option and as much notice as possible given.

If assessment has been rigorous and appropriate most candidates will know how they have got on almost immediately, and therefore they will recognise if the job isn't right for them. Alternatively, they will be full of expectation. Rejection, if fully understood with appropriate feedback, will do the brand no damage. Where they have no idea how they got on, because the selection had little link to the job, or the interviewer was unprepared, or asked trick questions, then damage is done. Where they think they've done ok and there is no feedback for an age, or ever about their performance, damage is done.

Delivering a good candidate experience is simple. Communicate, communicate, communicate. Be honest. Give feedback commensurate with the stage in the process the candidate has reached—if they are down to the last two after multiple stages, then they should get appropriate and full feedback. If they are rejected after CV application, a simple headline will do. For internal markets, this is just about treating colleagues with dignity. For the external brand, it's treating people and potential customers with dignity.

THE OFFER

As for the successful candidate, there is still a possibility to disappoint them after they have gone through selection. The offer should be easy. This is where everybody decides that everything is great and they want to commit. However, offer too little and it can prick the bubble of the candidate's enthusiasm. Offer too much and it can upset the pay balance in the team, have an overall upward pressure on the cost base, or give the new joiner nowhere to go as they advance and creates a problem in future years.

Everybody will have different policies and approaches to salary setting so, again, there is no right and no wrong way to do it. However, there are some basic principles to bear in mind. Don't reach a point of getting to the offer where the candidate is going to be surprised by what is in the envelope and you are going to be surprised by the reaction. Use data to inform the offer that is not purely based on the candidate's expectations. Make sure the offer is based on solid data—what the internal comparator is, what the market says and what the candidate is currently being paid. How you choose to interpret those pieces of data are organisation specific.

If there is a major mismatch in the data between the candidate and team and market, at least you know which problem to choose. Internal moves are often governed by rules about the level of pay rises that are self-defeating in the long run. An arbitrary figure about the level of increase for an internal candidate, or a rule that the pay increase will be managed in the next pay cycle leaves a bad taste. External hires that join on more can upset the team. Poor reward decisions have consequences.

The key thing is that by the time you get to offer, the candidate should have been maintained at a level of excitement. The job is what they want, the organisation is where they want to be and they have a really good idea of what the total package will be. You should know, before you get to the offer about current package and expectation and what the job value is. *No surprises* is always a good thought to hold at this stage.

ONBOARDING

The onboarding into the organisation is something that is frequently overlooked, but not difficult to manage well, and can be a spectacular own goal if mismanaged. After all the hard work of brand building and assessing and getting that offer right, you need to exploit the enthusiasm and good fuzzy feeling the new joiner has on day one and beyond. A survey by the Aberdeen Group reported that 86% of respondents felt that a new hire's decision to stay with a company long term is made within the first six months of employment. That puts the importance of onboarding into clear perspective. The Harvard Business Review, June 2017, in the article "Your New Hires Won't Succeed Unless You Onboard Them Properly", suggests that companies lose 17% of employees in the first six months. All that work, and then it's start again.

That same study suggests that being socially accepted is the key. There are other factors that are even lower down the hierarchy of needs that too often are overlooked. Desk space, a laptop, a phone, knowing what the dress code is, time to start, name of supervisor. It's crazy, but just about everyone you speak to will have their own personal story about a first day in a new job that was sensationally terrible, and utterly avoidable.

There is the period between the offer having been accepted and the candidate starting, as they work out their notice. That is a great time to either make the new employee feel great about joining, or to leave them in a vacuum of uncertainty. It really isn't difficult to do the former either. That is simple communication, providing necessary information.

The Commonwealth Games in Glasgow provided a great example of how this period can be managed at low cost for volume hiring. They had hundreds of customer service staff all starting on the same day and staff shortages could have been a desperately poor start to the showpiece games. They had also completed the recruitment for these staff months before they were needed. That could be a problem. So, they established social media forums, diarised time for line managers to check-in. Made sure they did it. Checked that all the starters knew what they needed to know and made them feel comfortable about day one. It was not complicated but it was communication with every individual. The result was that they had 100% attendance on the first day.

Part of that wasn't because everybody stayed engaged for the months leading to the games. It was a long period and these were entry-level jobs, so many people got other jobs in the time period. However, because the team was focused all the way on engagement, they knew when people were dropping out and could backfill the gaps.

The trouble is that too often, once the offer has been sorted, the task is considered complete and the hiring manager will get back to the day job. Naturally, they are extremely busy and the intention to keep in touch with the new person is lost in the hurly-burly of getting things done. This is an opportunity to start the onboarding and socialising before the person enters the building. Once you have a great person coming to join, full of enthusiasm, that effort is worth it to get a highly motivated and comfortable joiner.

What people need when they do join will vary from role to role and from individual to individual, but there are some elements that form the basis of all great onboarding programmes. There is a difference according to the stage in the career, with people at an early stage needing more confidence supporting activity and clear help with the company and the role. Joiners at more senior levels will have different levels of expectation and different needs, but all the research tells us the same thing about onboarding.

New joiners who receive a structured onboarding programme are more likely to stay and be more productive sooner. It makes sense—happy and engaged people are more likely to perform. There is no single right way to onboard people, but there are basic principles to think about.

There needs to be a structure. It must be something that doesn't start and end on day one, but have a plan for the first week, month and even beyond. Organisations that invest in onboarding and offer leading-edge onboarding programmes like LinkedIn, Google and Facebook all recognise that good onboarding can stretch to three or six months in, even if it's just a "How are you getting on?" at the later stages.

Make a good first impression, and make that first impression about the team and the environment. A first week filling in forms and trawling the intranet will stick in the mind for all the wrong reasons. Technology that doesn't work will be talked about. Having to borrow a security pass from someone they've never met to go to the toilet is awful. Not knowing where they can go for lunch is awkward. Basic, common, unforgivable mistakes. This is easy. Get the basics right. Let the new joiner know who they should know, and why they should know them. Help them understand the culture and politics.

At entry level it can be as simple as who do they ask for on day one? What time do they show up at? What training do they get? What is the dress code? What are the breaks? Where is lunch? Who is going to show them around?

Ensure the basics are in place and build a proper plan to socialise and integrate the individual into the organisation. Who they need to know and how they get things done.

At executive level help them understand the background of their peers. Who manages what. What the culture is. What the strategy is. Key barriers, key opportunities. Who are they meeting and why? The senior joiner will also need to play a key role in shaping their own onboarding and the structure will be different for each individual.

Whatever the level, it doesn't take a massive leap of imagination to put yourself in the shoes of that new joiner and think about what they will need and want in their early days with the business. However, the leap is to get leadership and management to recognise the importance of the activity and the positive and negative impact. Yet again, the culture surrounding resourcing activity is the key barrier, or enabler for success.

The *how* will vary from business to business; if this is something that is managed through technology, a series of managerial checklists, owned by an HR manager or specific to each business unit. It is, however, something that is too important, too easily forgotten or dismissed and frankly too easy to get right, to be left to the vagaries of chance. It needs an owner to make sure that it happens or to get it done, and for new employees to get help or even suggest improvements.

18F is an office within the General Services Administration of the US Government that collaborates with other agencies to fix technical problems, build products, and improve how government serves the public through technology. When they wanted to improve their new candidate onboarding process in a period of high growth in 2014, it was only logical that they would use technology to solve the problem of how to get a great deal of information to their new starters.

It's a highly technical environment and new starters in different areas need to have individualized training blocks early on, as well as company-wide information.

So, to solve the problem, the designers broke it into modules and augmented their knowledge of what new joiners would want by asking directors and leads a number of questions:

- What do you want every new hire on your team to know?

- When is the first time you talk to a new hire on your team?

- What tools do you use to share information with your team?

- What should 18F teach every new hire, regardless of team?

- Who does onboarding well outside of 18F?

They created a bot to manage onboarding, which pushed information to the new joiners in a programmed schedule to avoid information overload. Best of all, because they are a US Government agency and know their West Wing trivia, they called the bot Mrs. Landingham.

In 2012 Boston Consulting Group conducted a survey to understand which HR activities had the strongest link to company profitability. They concluded that onboarding came second of twenty-two core activities. That was ahead of leadership development, management training, diversity and strategic workforce planning. This is important.

What did they conclude was number one on their list? Recruitment delivery.

CHAPTER 13
THE FUTURE

"Great things in business are never done by one person. They're done by a team of people."

Steve Jobs

A year after undertaking the Lothian Bank capability review, James was driving home while reflecting on another challenging day. One of their competitors had dropped a rate on their headline mortgage product, and were heavily marketing. James suspected they were fattening themselves up for sale, but that was largely irrelevant as the impact on Lothian Bank was being felt immediately. It was a worrying assault on their most profitable product.

Sally, the operations director, had briefed him that morning. There had been a surge in call volumes as customers wanted termination quotes, or were asking for a matching rate. Fortunately, despite the unexpected volumes, they could cope. They were finally at full strength for permanent staff, and Sally knew the local temp supplier could now easily supply any additional heads they required as they hadn't soaked up the temp market. She was confident about holding customer satisfaction levels, as there was a marked improvement in call handling.

Tom, the head of mortgages, had his team modelling some responses to the situation and although he doubted if they could match on all fronts, the immediate headline was that the impact could be managed. It was still a concern and they would have the data to look at the next day. James reflected on how much the guy had come on. Following the meeting with the regulator and his conversation with Chris, James got some support in for Tom. He'd really turned the corner, and James knew that was because he had seen that something needed to be done with the situation and tackled it.

James reflected on how things had changed for him. It was just over a year ago that he started to get the sense that all was not well. In fact, he was moving from issue to issue and constantly firefighting. All part of the job. But was it? As he thought about it deeply at the heart of each of his issues there was some sort of people issue, and it all seemed to boil down to not having the right person with the right skills in place in time. Or having someone in place who wasn't quite up to the mark.

He didn't even know what the problem was. Up to the point he thought about, he didn't know there was a problem at all. Isn't this just the way of it? It felt like a crisis. He had severe doubts about the ability of the Bank to deliver the growth plan.

He remembered that they felt on edge with their whole customer service operation. It felt as though it was constantly teetering on the brink of a major collapse. He felt exposed about the lack of high-quality cybersecurity people in place. He knew hackers were targeting banks, and he felt they were vulnerable. He knew that head office was a difficult place to get things done. Most acutely he felt he had made a list of compromises with his top team. Compromises in areas he hadn't intended to make. He felt that deeply. Individually each compromise was acceptable, but cumulatively it built up.

That was when Chris had come to him with her list of proposals to address these issues, and for the long term.

She shone a light into the dark corners of how they thought about people. How the whole organisation went about putting resources in place. Basically, there was no conscious thought involved. They just ploughed on and didn't ever stop and question why they were doing what they were doing. What was the best way to think about capability, and what did they need to do to secure a better future? It was all in the moment, all reactive, and all in silos. They had problems they didn't know they had and were missing opportunities they didn't know existed.

It was different now. They made conscious decisions about how they wanted to resource the business. They had certainly felt the difference in certain areas. Straight away that morning with the mortgage problem, James felt instant calm that the customer service team would manage their challenge. He had more trust in his senior team to respond well to any crises. He reflected on the tough choices they'd made and the risks they'd taken in promoting two people to the executive team from the talent pool. He was proud that they did that, and proud of how the team now worked together.

It hadn't been easy. Change meets resistance, and particularly change when it comes to people and people management. But Chris had a strategic plan for capability. It reflected the business plan, so all the leaders got behind it, and they could see how it made sense to get the right skills lined up. That meant that Chris's team had to step up though, and he knew that HR had really changed how they did things. Much better for managers, and better results already. He felt a glow of satisfaction as he saw the real improvements all around him.

James just felt assured that they would continue to move forward with capability, and that gave him confidence that all problems would be overcome. His own team was coming together and they were starting to make comforting noises about what they were getting from HR. It was early, but it was all good.

Chris and Lucy had just finished Lucy's annual review and had gone out for dinner to celebrate what had been a great start to her career at Lothian Bank. The job was far from done, but progress had been immense. Having James as a key supporter and sponsor of the work certainly didn't hurt, but Chris recognised that Lucy's forward thinking and passion for the candidate was infecting the whole team.

They talked at length about the challenges they had faced, and how things were and just how badly the whole HR function had been viewed. There was no lack of desire in the business to have the right resource in place, they just didn't know how to do it. It wasn't something that was seen as a priority, and any issues were dealt with in isolation.

The frenetic nature of the non-stop recruitment in the contact centres was forcing the business into making quality compromises all the time. They had no clear appreciation of what the quality *bar* should be, they just kept rolling people in. That created a raft of problems and recruitment was seen as the problem, not the way to solve things. That was the first major step of improvement.

Head office recruitment had been worse, and there was little internal mobility to help. It was an expensive and variable thing. The most frustrating thing was that individually no manager was aware of the cumulative impact of all the compromises that were being made. The organisation was barely aware of their slide to mediocrity. They just assumed it was the way things were. As HR director, Chris was horrified at the moment in the capability review when she realised that she hadn't been all over it. That was a stomach-churning thought.

As for talent management, Chris realised that it was causing harm rather than good. It was frustrating the high-potential, high-performing people on the talent programmes and the executive didn't ever see the benefit or the point. Of all the things to act as a demotivator that was a strange one, but that's precisely what it did. In addition, they couldn't keep their graduates, and that meant that managers didn't see the benefit, which meant they didn't prioritise them, which meant they kept losing them. An expensive, vicious circle.

James getting fully behind the need to plan, and then his endorsement of the uncomfortable messages in the plan, was invaluable. His leadership team had followed. Chris and Lucy had completed the strategic capability and workforce plan quite quickly, and developed the action plan to deliver for the future. That was when it seemed too much and overwhelming.

However, Lucy had delivered. Chris had changed her structure, combining the recruitment and talent teams together into a resourcing function, under Lucy. She also tasked her with getting the mix right as the plan had indicated, and that meant ramping up internal mobility. It was a big ask. One that she stepped up to.

Lucy was very happy with her first year, but also immensely relieved. She had feared that James would want to outsource the lot, or want HR taken out of the process as he felt they had failed. His backing was something that galvanised her efforts and made her determined to succeed. It also slightly terrified her that the CEO wasn't losing any interest in her expanded department at all, and she had had one or two adrenaline-fuelled presentations to the executive over the year, starting with the employer branding work. She shuddered inside when she thought that things could have been so very different.

The function she inherited was full of very competent people, but they were demoralised and struggled to deliver real benefits for the business. Recruitment was seen as something anyone could do, without any expertise, and had become administrators filling in documentation. They were held to account for measures that actually forced down an emphasis on quality, and they were delivering a candidate experience that must have been costing them customers. Overstretched and undervalued. If it hadn't been for James's drive to change and Chris's enthusiasm, that would still be the case. But things had changed and were definitely moving in the right direction.

They invested in redoing the supplier branding work with a new supplier. It focused first on the contact centre recruitment and later they did separate work for head office. The output *felt* right, but more importantly it had immediate impact. Staff related to it, and they improved the level of awareness and interest externally very quickly.

Lucy now had a great relationship with Sally in operations. They had worked hard together and the new process was much better. There were still days at the assessment centre when all candidates bombed, but overall the ratios were better, quality better, new joiners happier. The numbers were now good, and the reliance on temporary staff was behind them.

Importantly, Lucy felt her team was now much more valued for the work they did and she enjoyed the sense of partnership they had with operations. The planning was still unpredictable, but rather than fight it they were building slack into the system.

They had struggled initially to get what they knew they needed in head office, but eventually won the argument. The fact that all the spend was based on a vacancy-by-vacancy decision was driving costs high, but although the managers doing the recruitment were convinced they were securing quality from agency hiring, the opposite was the case. Without the investment to build the branding communities for each area all they were doing was a distress purchase each time. They were making compromises in their choices they hadn't planned to make. Assessment was so patchy as to be a coin toss as to whether the new hire was of the right quality.

They centralised the candidate attraction and were working on training the managers. They'd also really strengthened the screening and worked on the governance, but this was always going to be a tough environment to illustrate the improvement in quality over the short term. Fortunately, they were already making savings, and time to hire was reducing, so that vindicated their case.

The real big, early win was the discovery of the need to build a long-term pipeline for some specialist areas. That changed the focus of their graduate recruitment push and, as well as a leadership programme for graduates, they now had the digital graduate programme and other parts of the business were looking for their own streams. That was very exciting.

There were many things that they had taken on— promoting the internal jobs market, addressing the graduate programme, executive assessment, use of temps and many other small projects. It sometimes felt like a mountain to climb, but they both felt they were now doing something that was contributing to business success and not just filling in forms.

As she headed home after the dinner with Chris, Lucy allowed herself a smile. It certainly wasn't a year she had been expecting, but it had been a lot of fun. Many late nights and a load of stress, but once they started to change things she relished that the pressure was now on her to deliver. They had delivered, and it was recognised. She had been in the spotlight and things had gone well. They had a plan, they had sponsorship and they had put a huge focus on delivering a great service to managers and candidate experience.

Strategic resourcing is making conscious decisions about how you will resource a business to deliver the business plan. The opportunities for competitive advantage are crystal clear. "The team with the best players wins."

Its success is dependent on three critical conditions. There is no shortcut either. The absence of one will eventually undermine the other two, and the benefits will be tactical. Combined, the benefits are long term and strategically important.

There is the need for a long-term capability plan, or strategic workforce plan. Tied to the business plan and with a long horizon. That gives you the information to make informed decisions. Build or buy, temporary or permanent, outsource, offshore, etc. It also tells you what you need for your delivery operating model. That is an essential enabling condition.

There is excellence in delivery. Delivery that has the customer/candidate/staff member/high-potential talent individual in mind. Building the brand, excellent attraction, rigorous assessment and common-sense onboarding.

Movement and changes in organisations provide an opportunity for resource design. A constant opportunity to challenge yourself about the capability of the business. If that is a promotion, or external hire or a contractor, the secret to making resourcing a key business enabler and driver is to make conscious and informed decisions. That establishes credibility, that illustrates results.

The other condition is a company culture that embraces strategic resourcing.

What does that culture look like? It is unique to each organisation, but shares some basic themes. An understanding that resourcing or recruitment is an important activity. A recognition that there is an expertise that surrounds it, which is based on science, experience and judgement. An acceptance of personal limitations. A treatment of candidates like they are the most valued of customers. An understanding that recruitment, like all strategic business activities needs thoughtfulness, planning and knowledge.

It isn't the responsibility of the business leadership, or the line managers in every department to suddenly understand this is the case. They have their own important things to deliver, and recruitment is just a small portion of a day job. HR needs to lead the way. However, it will not be successful as just an HR initiative. Everyone with a management responsibility needs to understand the difference they make. The importance of getting resourcing right. Right from the top. Especially from the top.

HR can unlock potential of an organisation through developing a more strategic approach to resourcing the business. Having the right people in the right place at the right time prevents problems at source and creates opportunities. The beneficial impact of investing in getting resourcing right is literally impossible to measure. That's not hyperbole.

The burden of convincing people that this is a goal worth pursuing is not an easy one. Everyone in the business has a solid case for investment. Marketing can point to greater revenue. Operations can point to efficiencies. Production can point to an increase in output. With resourcing, cash invested *over here* yields a multitude of benefit *over there*. It isn't a straight-line ROI. You can calculate time saved for mangers in fewer interviews, you can point to a reduction in short-term tenure, you can showcase the number of graduates that stay the course. They scratch the surface of the real benefits, and don't really stand up well to comparison in the case for investment in other departments. Tangible as they are though, they are superficial and minor benefits when compared with the real prize.

Changing culture is so often a change in mindset and belief from the leadership. Where they cannot envisage the return on investment, where they cannot see a straight line to revenue growth, where they can only see a function that is a cost, you have a challenge. Moreover, you are convincing them to back something that is undefinable. The work to improve will not mean a magical overnight shift, but will mean that the probability of filling every single vacancy with the best choice is higher than it was before. You are selling the cumulative effect of the increase in probability of thousands of events being better. Difficult to measure, but the prize is greater than just about anything else that could demand investment.

Have the right people in the right place at the right time doing the right things and you avoid the problems you know about. You seize the opportunities you know about. What you really do though is avoid the problems you will now never know about and create opportunities that were not imagined.

The leadership must understand and endorse the need for the strategic capability planning, beyond numbers for finance. There needs to be a recognition that the branding isn't selling a job today, it's building a community for tomorrow. Comprehension that assessment isn't pure science and isn't gut feel. A desire to ensure that the person who joins the team is fired up and feels great on day one, at the end of week one, six months in. That isn't something that happens by accident.

Making a conscious decision about resourcing is making a conscious decision to be better. Choosing how you resource your business with skills and attitudes is choosing your future. Plan for the long term, execute with passion and precision, and bring the business with you. Grasp that better future.

JOHN WALLACE

www.resourcinginsights.co.uk
https://www.linkedin.com/in/john-wallace-87b5261/

John Wallace has worked in the recruitment business for over 20 years. He started his recruitment career with an independent consultancy in Scotland, he went on to work in resourcing leadership and senior HR roles with RBS, Tesco and Barclays. Since 2015 he has consulted with a variety of businesses providing diagnosis for problems and insight for solutions.

Over the years, John has been responsible for the recruitment of tens of thousands of people, developed innovative hiring processes, created award-winning campaigns, driven change and delivered recruitment that delivered results for businesses. His experience has been across the globe, and working through the arc of resourcing activity.

Through this experience John has seen the damage that poor resourcing can do to a business and the huge benefits of getting it right. Yet, too often, resourcing only receives focus and investment in times of crisis. John is passionate about the need for resourcing to be though of as a critical activity in a business environment that is changing more rapidly, and dramatically than ever. He advocates a strategic approach to resourcing that is more than filling jobs. Thinking about the future, and not just short-term execution.

John lives in Edinburgh and still can't putt.

BUSINESS TITLES FROM MPOWR

Mission: Leadership

Ben Morton

ISBN: 9781907282713

Your Slides Suck!

David Henson

ISBN: 9781907282782

The Key—To Business and Personal Success

Martyn Pentecost

ISBN: 9781907282171

THE PUBLISHER'S GUIDE SERIES

The Heist: Cracking the Marketing Code Through Authoring a Book

ISBN: 9781907282249

Write Your Book, Grow Your Business

ISBN: 9781907282546

Storyselling Your Business

ISBN: 9781907282591

27118111R00118

Printed in Great Britain
by Amazon